The
Gift of
Anger

The Gift of Anger

Ruth Wilson

BRISTOL BOOKS®

WILMORE, KY 40390

THE GIFT OF ANGER:
How God Helps Us Face and Overcome Our Conflicts
© 1990 by Ruth Wilson
Published by Bristol Books

First Edition, August 1990

Unless otherwise indicated, all Scripture quotations are from the *Holy Bible*, the New International Version, © 1973, 1978, 1984 by the International Bible Society. Used by Permission.

Scripture quotations indicated (AMP) are from the *Amplified Bible*.

Author's Note: The persons described in this book are composites and do not represent any one specific person. Their conversations and problems represent typical situations encountered in Emotional Expression Therapy sessions. We hope readers will be able to identifiy with these examples and apply the solutions to their lives.

ISBN: 0-917851-56-0

Printed in the United States of America

BRISTOL BOOKS
An Imprint of Bristol, Inc.
P.O. Box 150 • 308 East Main Street • Wilmore, KY 40390
Phone: 606/858-4661—Fax: 606/858-4972

CONTENTS

Foreword

"It doesn't seem right to me for those guys to get that angry with each other. After all, we're seminarians," I said. The senior upperclassman smiled. "When you're living in an atmosphere charged with love, there is bound to be tension." he said.

Over the years I have discovered the truth of his observation. Anger happens because we care. In a caring community we can expect heated conversations from time to time. That is not the problem. The problem is knowing what to do about the discharge of emotion.

"Christians don't get angry," I falsely assumed. That means when anger erupts it is necessary to deny and suppress it or suffer rejection for giving vent to it.

"'In your anger do not sin': Do not let the sun go down while you are still angry," is what the Bible tells us to do (Ephesians 4:26). When people live in relationship and care for each other it is inevitable that from time to time tempers flare or disagreements surface. So far no sin. It is only when we cut the other person off and pretend he or she no longer exists that sin enters in. We are obligated to resolve our anger before the setting sun.

That is more easily said than done. I only wish I had known the insights of this book by Ruth Wilson when I began my ministry almost 40 years ago. It would have enabled me to be more effective in the ministry of reconciliation (2 Corinthians 5:18,19). I have known broken marriages that might have been saved if the couples had learned to fight fairly. I have known of severed church relationships that might never have happened if all concerned had been willing to resolve differences before darkness.

Ruth has candidly written of herself. She has lucidly described many situations she has experienced in her career as an emotional therapy counselor. She has generously shared her invaluable insights. She writes as a committed Christian. She has expressed authentic Christian wisdom. Such wisdom is of great benefit to all human beings, regardless of personal spiritual convictions.

"When you're living in an atmosphere charged with love, there is bound to be tension." True, and may the insights of this book enable all who read it resolve the anger born of tension and deepen the relationship of love.

The Reverend Don Stivers

Introduction

Anger is a strong emotion that affects us all, yet we are often baffled by what to do with it. Everywhere I go people want to know more about anger. I have spent years searching for ways to make my anger work. This book answers some of our questions about this powerful emotion. As the founder of the Emotional Expression Therapy Center, I have dedicated my life to doing God's work by helping people learn to genuinely love one another. I believe a deep level of sincere love is impossible unless we are willing to constructively disagree with each other and hassle through our problems. Anger, hurt and love are our primary feelings, and they are tied together. We can't have love without anger and hurt, though we often wish we could.

Anger is the key to the inner person. Underneath our anger lies our protected hurt, which is equally important to share. If we learn to accept our anger and hurt as important and necessary, and if we learn to express these feelings appropriately, *then* we will experience deep love in our intimate relationships.

Next to our relationship with God, the people who are closest to us are our greatest source of comfort and joy. God wants us to have committed, permanent relationships, and he has built into us a range of feelings which enable us to reach that purpose. When we open up the channels of our feelings, we experience God's love flowing through our emotions to strengthen our intimate relationships.

What prevents expressions of anger, hurt and love? Our greatest barriers to anger expression come from hurts experienced early in childhood. We watched destructive fighting in our homes, or we felt the tension of unexpressed anger between our parents. I remember fearing that something terrible would happen when Mom and Dad argued. We got the message that anger was bad, and we decided early to avoid expressing disagreements. Because we learned to distrust our feelings, we are *afraid* to risk expressing them.

The good news is that anger can be a gift—if it is thoughtfully and carefully wrapped and shared. Respectfully telling those we love what is bothering us is an invitation to know and understand us. If I tell you why I'm angry I feel much more *me* and more connected to you. Expressing anger is an invitation to love more deeply.

Much can be said about anger and its expression. I have spent my entire life learning from God about my own anger expression and the consequences of it. My anger was out of control during my childhood. I remember my mother frowning and shaking her head over my outbursts. Uncurbed, my anger as an adult gave me bad feelings about myself. In fact, I almost lost my marriage to destructive expressions of anger.

As a Christian, the Bible verses about anger made sense to me, but I had trouble distinguishing good anger from bad. When I finally learned that the exhortation to "be angry but do not sin" meant harnessing my anger, my emotions began to work *for* me rather than *against* me. I felt wonderful. The light bulb went on. Eventually I felt called to be a professional counselor and teacher of emotional expression.

This book was written to guide you in establishing a good, safe arena in which to share disagreements with those closest to you. These principles have evolved from years of personal life experience, training and counseling others. I thank my family, my staff, my church family and my clients for their help as God has shaped my spirit through the experience of writing this book. I have been transformed in the process and have come to trust him, to depend on him and to humbly thank him for what you are about to receive.

Ruth Wilson
Santa Barbara, California
1990

Chapter One

Open Your Angry Heart

*"Therefore, each of you must put off falsehood
and speak truthfully to his neighbor, for we are all
members of one body. In your anger do not sin: Do
not let the sun go down while you are still angry, and
do not give the devil a foothold."*

Ephesians 4:25-27

I was an angry child and my anger got me into lots of
trouble. Once my big sister made me so mad that I threw my
hair brush at her. Another time a playmate wouldn't give me
a ride in his kiddy car as he had promised, so I hit him on
the head with a toy rake, opening a bleeding cut. My sister
cried as she dragged me home. When my parents heard the
story they pulled down the shades and locked the door,
fearing retaliation from my playmate's family. I was
surprised and shocked at their actions, and I felt like a bad
person.

No one spoke directly to me about how to handle my
anger as a child. But I did receive an unspoken message:
Anger is bad and I was bad for being angry. So I tried to
control my anger. I would count to ten, bite my tongue and
even lie about my feelings. Sometimes I held my temper for
weeks or even months. Then—*wham!*—something would go
wrong, and I would see red and fly into a rage.

When I married at age 18, I carried my moody, unpredictable anger into our new relationship. I tried hard to please my husband, Jack. But disappointments and disagreements often triggered my anger, which I expressed as icy indifference or blazing retribution. After every angry outburst I felt like a failure. I was out of control, and I didn't like myself.

As our family grew, I often misplaced my anger with Jack by yelling at the children. With each such episode my self-esteem sank lower. In the fourteenth year of our marriage, I resolved not to lose my temper or raise my voice for one entire year. I am a strong-willed person, and I almost succeeded. But I felt miserable all year and kept getting sick.

Finally, Jack and I sought counseling. One day at a workshop on anger, a brilliant sun of hope burst through the clouds of my despair. I realized for the first time that my anger was not bad, even though my expression of it was usually wrong. I trembled with joy when I began to realize that anger could be positive! I learned that expressing my anger in proper ways could help develop closeness in my relationship with Jack and the children instead of driving us farther apart.

It was a life-changing moment for me. I am convinced our marriage was saved by the counseling I received. I began to see my anger as a gift from God instead of a devilish goad. I felt better about myself.

The timely workshop was an example of God's gracious direction and sovereign intervention in our lives. My life-changing moment developed into a fulfilling career as a God-centered counselor teaching emotional expression.

Anger in Perspective

Ephesians 4:25-27 tells us that all Christians can expect to feel angry at times. It's an honest, God-given, human emotion. We are told to say the truth to the person we're feeling angry with, but we are cautioned not to respond to the emotion of anger in a sinful way. We need to explain what bothers us without discrediting the other person. We are not to let anger fester. Rather Scripture tells us to deal with it right away. If we don't, it could cause judgments, grudges and rejection. The devil relishes those opportunities to get a foothold in our lives. We need to use our anger as a commitment to be together and close to other people. Our response to anger can either make or break our relationships. If anger is to be a positive gift in our lives we must do more than just feel it. We need to say we are angry, resentful, bothered and upset. The emotion of anger must be combined with constructive thoughts and appropriate decisions. The word *anger* often frightens us needlessly. Throughout this book we will define anger as a strong feeling of displeasure. Anger only gets us into trouble when we allow it to boil to the surface unchecked where it explodes as judgment or violence, or if we swallow it and withdraw. Instead of these responses to anger, we must evaluate the feeling of displeasure, thoughtfully identify its source and creatively choose a proper way to express it. In a relationship we must express the displeasure we feel instead of burying it. This is necessary to stay open to each other and truly love one another as the Lord asks.

Let Your Insides Out

Most counselors, both Christian and non-Christian, agree that intimate relationships such as marriages and close friendships require the open and honest expression of feelings, including anger. Bottled up anger and resentment cause numerous problems from high blood pressure to divorce. The degree to which counselors recommend that anger should be expressed ranges from politeness to passionate yet constructive forthrightness, which is my perspective.

Our feelings make us alive and vibrant. They are a wholesome, God-given part of us. As with all our emotions, we need to let our feelings of displeasure out or they will eat us up inside. Feelings of love for a spouse are rightly expressed in words and deeds of caring, romance and love-making. Feelings of joy are correctly released through laughter, applause or shouts of "Hooray!" or "Praise the Lord!" Similarly, feelings of anger must be constructively stated for our own benefit and the benefit of those who are a part of what's bothering us. I encourage everyone to gradually learn to express their feelings of anger boldly and passionately. This gives zip to our lives.

In his pamphlet, *Anger,* Charles Swindoll discusses Paul's instructions concerning anger in Ephesians 4:26-27. Swindoll emphatically states that God is calling upon us to "be angry." He points out three important truths contained in these verses: "Anger is a God-given emotion. . . . Anger is not necessarily sinful. . . . Anger must have safeguards."[1] I could not agree more.

H. Norman Wright, in his book *Communication: Key to Your Marriage,* reminds us that Ephesians 4:31 says some expressions of anger must be put away. "Let all bitterness and indignation and wrath (passion, rage, bad temper) and resentment (anger, animosity) and quarreling (brawling, clamor, contention) and slander (evil-speaking, abusive or blasphemous language) be banished from you, with all malice (spite, ill will or baseness of any kind)" (AMP). Wright says, "It is important, however, to eventually talk about your anger. Somewhere, somehow, the anger has to be recognized and released in a healthy manner. Otherwise your storage apparatus will begin to overflow at the wrong time and the wrong place."[2]

We come to an important distinction in the expression of anger: "Anger is emotional energy that may be directed to accomplish good (indignation); however, uncontrolled rage, passive hostility toward others, and resentment are all condemned as sin."[3] This book focuses on positive yet passionate ways to express anger for the purpose of accomplishing good.

The remainder of this chapter explores three main

reasons to express anger: anger is a gift from God and, like all God's gifts, it must be used properly; anger gives us individual strength; proper expression of anger helps develop intimate relationships.

Anger Is a Gift from God

God gets angry. When his people don't listen to him, God burns with anger. For example, 2 Kings 22:13 reads: "Go and inquire of the Lord for me and for the people and for all Judah about what is written in this book that has been found. Great is the Lord's anger that burns against us because our fathers have not obeyed the words of this book; they have not acted in accordance with all that is written there concerning us." Unlike human anger, God's anger is "the perfect wrath" because it only comes against that which is evil. God has righteous anger and only he can judge his people.

Jesus, in his sacred humanity, expressed righteous indignation. When he cleared the temple, for example, Jesus was openly angry: "In the temple court he found men selling cattle, sheep and doves, and others sitting at tables exchanging money. So he made a whip of cords, and drove all from the temple area, both sheep and cattle; he scattered the coins of the money-changers and overturned their tables. To those who sold doves, he said, 'Get these out of here!How dare you turn my Father's house into a market!'" (John 2:14-16). In Matthew 23 he expressed his anger at the hypocritical religious leaders, calling them "whitewashed tombs" (v. 27), "brood of vipers" (v. 33) and other names.

We also get angry. God has built into us every shade and degree of anger (as well as the other two basic emotions—hurt and warmth). Righteous, God-given anger is an asset if we respond to it properly.

We can't always trust our own motives, so it is important to pray, read God's Word and get feedback from our Christian friends. God has set the example for the proper expression of anger. We need to follow his example, using the Holy Spirit as our guide.

Jesus left us a sweeping directive: "A new commandment I give you: Love one another. As I have loved you, so you must love one another" (John 13:34). But Aunt Harriet is critical and hard to get along with. Brother Bob is an abusive alcoholic. A daughter refuses to attend church, saying she's not sure she believes in Jesus Christ. A husband works too hard and won't take time to say how he feels. Instead of loving these people as Jesus said, we become resentful, judgmental and angry. Love and anger appear to be on opposite ends of the scale.

But love and anger are not enemies; they are complementary gifts. We cannot truly love one another unless we keep the air clear by speaking our displeasure when issues arise. Jesus balanced John 13:34 with clear instructions for loving confrontation in Matthew 18:15: "If your brother sins against you, go and show him his fault, just between the two of you. If he listens to you, you have won your brother over." Jesus does not tells us to pussyfoot around the issue by hinting or to talk to others behind our brother's back.

This requirement to work out issues with each other is essential for our love to be sincere. If we cling to grudges we carry a heavy burden. On judgment day we will be accountable for how we handled our relationships. Our loving agreement, hammered out by expressing and resolving our displeasure, is a key to God's presence in our midst. God's love for us shines through in our deep love for each other. He gets right to the point with us, and we need to get right to the point with each other.

Anger Gives Us Individual Strength

Learning to understand and express anger well helps us view our anger as positive and constructive. Anger is a strong part of our personality. If properly channeled, our anger can become a creative and powerful force in our lives.

It gives us confidence and good self-esteem. Constructive anger makes us strong. We are agents for God, speaking out for him as he wants us to. On the other hand, destructive anger tears us down. It makes us feel ashamed and unworthy. Telling the truth is exciting. In voicing our disagreements we learn about ourselves and give those around us the opportunity to share in that knowledge. Our self-respect increases, and our honesty allows us to live more vital and fulfilling lives.

When we say more of what we're thinking and feeling we are the persons God intends us to be. Speaking our convictions, even at the risk of rejection, helps us clarify our beliefs and further develop our values. People respect us for our brave honesty. We are more dynamic and attractive when we have strong opinions and stand behind our convictions. There are times when we are called by God to speak out in righteous anger against sin.

Strength to Eliminate Fear

Anger is scary! Ninety nine and 99/100 percent of the people I know agree. Yet it is necessary to express anger. When we experience and express anger we discover we cannot be afraid and angry at the same time. The two feelings are incompatible. Sometimes we fluctuate between the two, yet the more angry we feel the less we are afraid. God does not want us to be timid or afraid. We are not to be doormats for others to walk upon. Jesus set the example for us by boldly speaking the truth even when his audience was hostile.

Our fear of confrontation will block us from effectively expressing our anger, but with practice we will be encouraged by our successes. Expressing anger really works. By pushing through the initial fear of confrontation, we develop the courage necessary to use our influence in the world. Our values will not prevail if we play it safe. If we take risks, we may be controversial, but we will also be respected.

Paul and Donna: Growing in Confidence. Donna was raised to believe that the husband rules the household. This is not the same as the biblical injunction for the husband to be the head of the household and to treat his wife as his own body. Many times her husband did what he wanted without taking into account her needs. Consequently, she had been afraid of her husband, Paul, especially when she disagreed with him and he became angry. But with prayer and support, Donna was able to overcome her fear and confront Paul at times when she strongly disagreed with his ideas.

"I applied for a consolidation loan today," Paul stated during dinner. "Now we can invest more money in the stock market."

Donna picked at her food anxiously. Mustering her courage, she responded, "I don't like this at all, Paul. We're sinking deeper into debt all the time. I think you're going too far by trying to make a big killing. I think you're being greedy."

Paul leaned forward angrily and countered, "This is my department, and I know what I'm doing. I've always taken care of you. I don't think I get enough credit for what I do."

"I do think you are a good provider," Donna continued. "And I probably don't give you enough credit. But in this instance I want you to listen to me. I am your partner and you need to consider my feelings. I don't want us to be so overextended."

Even though she felt afraid, Donna took a big step forward by voicing her strong opinion. Paul was understandably angry at first. This was a big change for him. But after subsequent discussions the couple was able to reach an amicable balance on the issue.

Paul had been afraid Donna would take over. His best defense was to be offensive. Donna assured him she didn't want to run things, she simply wanted to contribute her opinion to influence him.

As Donna gained the courage to voice her angry feelings,

her fear diminished. She began to feel more confident, her self-respect increased, and Paul began to respect her feelings more. They began to relax as they realized they had a strong impact on each other.

Strength to Release Tension

Our bodies suffer from fear of anger. When we become frozen with fear, tensions build up from the unexpressed anger. Prolonged tension produces physical problems such as headaches, hypoglycemia, high blood pressure, back trouble, insomnia, ulcers and a myriad of other stress-related ailments. Severe buildup can lead to cancer, heart attacks and death.

One great benefit of constructive anger expression is the sheer release of physical tension. When an argument is brewing, we feel nervous and uncomfortable. Once we begin to talk, the anxiety eases, and we are able to calmly engage in a good discussion. A healthy argument restores emotional and physical peace.

God is the Healer. He has shown me many times that when people say what bothers them their ailments improve. Holding onto bad feelings eats us up inside and gives the devil a foothold.

Teri and Lance: Tied Up by Tension. Teri and Lance both experienced physical tension before they allowed themselves the relief of an argument. Teri was restless, her heart race, and her breathing was shallow. Lance's muscles tightened, particularly in his lower back. The longer they withheld their anger, the more intense their symptoms became.

Finally the tension reached a breaking point. Lance reacted irritably by criticizing how Teri cleaned the stove.

"I'm sick and tired of how you pick on me for every little thing," Teri responded in a controlled voice. "I would like to go away alone this weekend just to get some peace and quiet."

"I don't get enough time with you as it is," Lance retorted, his voice deepening with anger. "I want you to stay home."

Teri riveted him with an angry look. "Who wants to be with you? You're so grouchy and bossy! You want me to do only what pleases you. I feel trapped. You don't own me."

By this time their self-consciousness was gone and they were fully absorbed in their fight. As they exchanged angry statements, their pent-up energy was released. Their anger dissipated, their tensions began to unwind, and the mood changed.

"I don't want to own you," Lance said quietly, feeling hurt. "I don't want you to spend every minute with me. I just need to know that you want to be with me."

Teri began to cry softly, "I do love you, Lance. I just get scared of you. I should say something sooner."

He took her in his arms for a long, relaxed hug. The tension was over.

Instead of pulling away and withdrawing, this time Teri had allowed herself to fully express her anger with Lance. What had been controlled and restrained became open and flowing, leading to close, caring feelings between them. Their angry exchange helped them relax and get in touch with their underlying hurt. Being vulnerable allowed their love to emerge.

Strength to Unlock Other Feelings

Each time Teri and Lance practiced arguing they trusted themselves more until a disagreement became "no big deal." Then they could permit themselves to go from anger into hurt into warmth. They no longer got stuck in anger.

This exchange between Teri and Lance illustrates the flow from one feeling to another. Each of us needs to accept and express all three of our basic feelings of anger, hurt and warmth in order to feel complete as a person. All three feelings are intertwined. Anger is on top. Expressing it leads us into the feeling of hurt, which in turn takes us deeper into warmth. We must accept anger, hurt and warmth as allies to succeed in handling the problems that confront us in our daily lives. Learning to express anger paves the way for the proper expression of hurt and warmth.

Conversely, to the extent that we stymie the expression of anger, we will find ourselves stymied in the proper expression of the feelings of hurt and warmth. We must develop the expression of all three. Since anger is often the most difficult to express constructively, mastering the expression of anger can facilitate success in the other two areas.

Expressing Anger Is the Key to Good Relationships

You cannot be in a close relationship for long without feeling some resentment. And you cannot remain close to the people dear to you unless you are willing to express your feelings of resentment and anger. If you do not express your feelings of irritation, they will smolder and ignite into a major conflict. Accumulated anger can eventually choke all the love out of a relationship.

A spoken resentment is a gift. We care so much about the other person that we want to share the truth of our feelings with him or her. We want to express what bothers us to dissolve the barrier between us. If your partner keeps telling you what bothers him or her, you know you are safe from rejection as a result of withheld anger and resentments. I used to fear arguing with my husband until I realized the intensity of his anger matched the intensity of his love. The more he told me what he didn't like the more I could trust him.

Speaking openly is also a way of becoming acquainted with each other. What better way is there to understand our individuality than to be direct about our irritations? It is a way of getting valuable information quickly.

Eric and Josie: Clearing the Air. Eric and Josie are newly married. They have already begun to practice voicing their irritations at the time they arise. Since they have not let problems build up, their anger is at a mild level.

Recently Eric and Josie were sitting together in front of the TV after a long day at work. "Josie, I don't like to sit around watching TV—it's boring," Eric said with an edge in his voice. "You'll fall asleep and go to bed early."

"I'm tired," Josie sighed. "I work hard all day. I wish you weren't so restless. You make me nervous. Relax," she said with an anxious laugh, pointing to the reclining chair.

Eric walked to the chair, hesitated, then sank into it. "I have a hard time relaxing. But I don't want to get into a rut. I want our time together to be special."

"I do too!" Josie affirmed. "Maybe I have been babying myself a bit. Living with you is a lot different from living alone." She smiled, turning toward Eric and away from the TV.

In this exchange Eric and Josie were open with and respectful of each other. They were learning how to be together and share information about themselves with each other. Since they care, they were listening and affecting each other. They were well on their way to achieving a healthy balance between the activity and relaxation they respectively prefer.

Rubbing Each Other the Right Way

One of the great joys of developing a relationship is the companionship which results from sharing feelings, reactions and opinions with each other. We value each other's viewpoints and are influenced by them.

As we spend time together we rub off on each other and become more harmonious. We have to trust we have power even if at first we seem miles apart. Perhaps some forty-five five-minute discussions later our patience will pay off, and we will see how we are beginning to agree. Eventually a separate relationship personality develops, drawn from our individual personalities.

Russ and Anna: Influencing Each Other. When Russ and Anna came to talk with me, they had just begun seeing each other. They were careful not to interfere with each other. They were polite, and each quietly endured annoyances with the other. Yet when I met with them separately, they had resentments to express. Russ complained that Anna was not exciting to be with. Anna complained that Russ did not express his feelings.

I appealed to them individually to take some risks, starting with having them ask what they wanted from each other. I had to convince them. Anna said she felt Russ had been hurt so much by his previous relationship that any request from her would create too much pressure for him. She was working on assumptions she had not checked out with Russ. Actually she was afraid to rock the boat because he might get angry.

Russ told me he thought Anna was too frightened to be more open with him. He also emphatically stated that he wanted her to give to him on her own, not out of compulsion.

"But how is she to know what you don't tell her?" I exclaimed. "I think you've seen too many Hollywood movies."

Russ was protecting himself. He was afraid Anna would get angry at him.

Because Russ and Anna were so careful and private about how they were feeling, they almost lost each other. Anna suggested they stay apart for awhile. Russ didn't want to stop seeing her. But instead of telling her that, he actually encouraged her to leave. With some encouragement, however, Russ decided to lay aside the mask of aloofness which covered up his fear.

"I do want you to stay!" Russ told Anna finally. "I think our relationship is good and I don't want to risk losing it. It's a blessing that we love each other."

"I can always come back if we miss each other so much, Russ," Anna assured him. "I still need to find out who I am."

"I think you can find out what you want when you're around me," Russ countered. "You don't need to go away to do that."

Anna left, but she was back in three weeks. She came back with enthusiasm to be close to Russ. Russ and Anna were able to deepen their relationship into marriage, yet they had almost lost each other because of their idealized thoughts about relationships.

Being Direct with One Another

In personal communications keeping our words simple and to the point works best. Unfortunately, we were taught to be mysterious and to play hard-to-get. Such games are a waste of time. I'm angry at the old adage that men are different from women and that we never will figure each other out. We have the same set of feelings—we all get angry, hurt and need love. We all stand to get more of what we want in a relationship by being direct with one another.

Mark and Nancy have trouble clearly stating what bothers them. Because of their fear of anger and their need to please each other they tiptoe around their irritations, increasing the frustration level for both of them.

Mark and Nancy: Pussyfooting Around Anger. Mark was on a ladder painting the ceiling as Nancy entered. "What's the matter, Nancy?" he asked with an edge in his voice. "You were going to help me on this painting project, but every time I turn around, you've disappeared."

"You know I need to take care of the kids," Nancy answered, feeling uneasy about the confrontation. Then she blurted out, "Besides, I haven't wanted to hang around you much."

Mark put down his brush and descended from the ladder. "Well, now that we're talking about it, I do resent that you wanted this project done. You want me to do all the work. That happens a lot. I think you just take me for granted."

"What bothers me is that you have to run this project totally your way," Nancy added boldly. "I would like to help if I could do it more my way."

Before letting down their guards, both of them were at opposite ends of the pole. Mark wanted help, and Nancy didn't want to give it. Once they were willing to express themselves directly they were able to consider each other's viewpoint.

They needed practice to build confidence so that arguing became a natural event instead of a trauma. After a few years they could take these exchanges in stride, and they gradually became relaxed companions.

Eliminating Judgments

As unspoken resentments fester and grow they become distorted, and we form a "case" against our partners. They are silently tried, judged and sentenced, deprived of the opportunity to defend themselves. We rob our loved ones and ourselves of fair discussion and a chance to understand what is going on.

A judgment is a hard and fast opinion. The judgments we hold against one another are first poured into our hearts like wet cement in the form of minor resentments. We must share our anger as soon as possible to prevent false judgments from hardening. Like cement, anger is much easier to deal with before it hardens.

Spontaneous expression does not mean that we blurt out our feelings without regard to the appropriate time and circumstances for ourselves and the other person. It takes just a few thoughtful seconds for us to evaluate the timing before speaking.

On the other hand, while we want to be considerate, we also want to avoid thinking about our feelings to the point of intellectualizing them and censoring the other person.

Rich and Jody: Uncorking Anger. Rich suffered from bottled up anger which caused him to become inwardly judgmental of his wife, Jody. He nursed his inner resentments toward her silently, but his negative attitude tipped her off. Jody was aware of Rich's moodiness and tackled the problem.

"I'm not feeling close to you, Rich, and I don't know what's wrong," Jody said, breaking an uncomfortable silence. "You don't want to talk, and I'm getting so I don't look forward to being with you."

After a long pause Rich reluctantly stated, "Well, I'm having serious doubts about our marriage. I've been thinking it over, trying to decide what I want to do."

Jody, becoming animated, angrily replied, "I wish you had told me what you were thinking instead of keeping it all to yourself until you want to get rid of me. No wonder I feel insecure with you!"

Rich turned to her with resolve and stated in a rush, "I'm not having enough time with you, and you're not even glad to see me. You don't want to have sex. Sometimes you don't even want to sleep with me. It bugged me when you said you couldn't spend time with me because of your work, and then you slept until noon. I don't think you're being mature or responsible."

Jody began to cry. Through her tears she said, "I feel overwhelmed. I feel like you don't like me at all."

Rich had allowed his resentments to build until he felt like rejecting Jody. He had felt tense and unhappy, lying awake at night and anxious during the day. Feeling overwhelmed by such a long list of criticisms, Jody found it difficult to respond when she finally learned their marriage was in jeopardy.

Their anxiety and grief could have been prevented if they had addressed the issues one at a time as they developed and then let go of them after their feelings had been expressed.

During counseling Rick explored why he was afraid to

mention annoyances whenever they occurred. Some of the answers lay in his dysfunctional family background. Because of his alcoholic parents, anger was expressed in ugly ways. Rick also needed to recognize the alcoholic patterns of being crisis-oriented and looking at situations as either black or white.

Jody began to understand her role as co-dependent. Her life hung on Rick's mood, and if he were angry with her she felt wiped out. As they both discovered why they lacked the ability to express their anger well, their fear gradually subsided. Prayer for God's healing of their early life traumas led them to be braver in saying what bothered them.

We have covered three main reasons why we should express anger. First, anger is given to us by God and he wants us to express it righteously as he does. Expressing anger constructively helps us to fulfill Jesus' command to love one another.

Second, anger expression gives us inner strength as individuals. Openness about our angry feelings helps us overcome fear, release inner tension and relate to our other feelings.

Third, expressing anger enables us to have good relationships. It gives us the ability to understand each other on a deep level, giving us the freedom to be close and loving.

Now that the purpose of anger is clear, let us prepare to express it!

Notes

1. Charles Swindoll, *Anger* (Portland, OR: Multnomah Press), pp.6-7.

2. H. Norman Wright, *Communication: Key to Your Marriage* (Ventura, CA: Regal Books), p. 88.

3. Ben Chapman, *NIV Counselor's New Testament and Psalms* (Grand Rapids, MI: Zondervan Bible Publishers), p. 461.

Chapter Two

Drawing the Line on Anger

"A patient man has great understanding, but a quick-tempered man displays folly."

Proverbs 14:29

Now that we have discovered the positive reasons for expressing our anger, we need to understand the limits for expressing it. It is good for us to admit that we are angry, but we don't want to alienate the people around us. Proverbs 14:29 points out that we are not to pounce on people with our anger. Instead, we are to thoughtfully consider the situation before we speak out. Ephesians 4:25-27 allows room for the expression of anger. But Ephesians 4:31 instructs, "Get rid of all bitterness, rage and anger, brawling and slander, along with every form of malice." All bad anger is to be put aside and the good anger expressed.

What is the acceptable middle ground between suppression and rage? What are the boundaries between constructive and destructive anger? How do we know when we are hurting instead of helping ourselves and others in the expression of anger?

The boundaries for anger are often obscure to us because we mistakenly install ourselves as judges over those who wrong us and spark our anger. Pride and selfish motives drive us to lash out to right the wrong. But Paul wrote, "Do not take revenge, my friends, but leave room for God's wrath, for it is written: 'It is mine to avenge, I will repay,' says the Lord" (Romans 12:19). God is the only one who can judge fairly since his anger never oversteps its bounds. We are allowed to say we are angry and state what bothers us—period. We are called to tell the truth about how we feel. That's as far as we're supposed to go. Judgment for wrong suffered and changes in those who offend us are up to God, the righteous Judge.

Another reason we have trouble keeping our anger in bounds is our tendency to get angry too fast. Proverbs cautions us to tame a quick temper with patience (see Proverbs 14:29; 15:18; 16:32). When a dam bursts, the water which tumbles down the canyon is impossible to control. But the same water can be productively released gallon by gallon through the dam's monitored pumping system. In the same way, we need to monitor and release the reservoir of our anger carefully so that it will not gush over its boundaries.

Sometimes we become panicky because we don't trust ourselves and our anger. We overdo our anger when we feel helpless. I have to remind myself that I do have power and influence even if the person I'm talking to is not acknowledging me. I'm expressing myself, and I'm influencing them in the long run. I lose my effectiveness if I let my anger take over. When that happens, my point is lost, and I'm in the doghouse.

Being slow to anger implies that we must rely upon the Holy Spirit to monitor our thought and feeling processes. The emotion of anger must be combined with our intellect so we will be able to control the passion that might otherwise get us into trouble.

Putting Anger in Its Place

Webster's Concise Family Dictionary defines anger as "a strong feeling of displeasure." I like this definition because it reduces anger to a simple, manageable emotion. It is not too much to handle or too scary. Like other feelings, displeasure is not right or wrong in itself. It's what we do with our feelings that often gets us into trouble. When we talk about expressing our anger we're talking about communicating a feeling of displeasure. It should not be an explosion; it should be an exercise.

Many of the synonyms for anger are upsetting: wrath, ire, rage, fury, indignation. These words describe anger which is undisciplined, unchecked and out of bounds. They all indicate distorted anger which is always destructive in a relationship. Expressing feelings of displeasure through violence directed toward others is wrong. Instead, we should use clear, direct sentences when expressing angry feelings.

A positive, acceptable method for expressing feelings of displeasure is an argument. I define an argument as the exchange of negative information. Two or more people tell each other what they don't like and then drop the discussion. Arguments are seldom over black-and-white issues which can be settled by accumulating the proper facts. Their subjects are usually gray, springing from valid—but different—feelings, opinions or perspectives. Thus, a constructive argument has no winner and no loser. Each person must express displeasure openly and accept the expressed displeasure of the partner, then take time to digest the information.

As equals in an argument, each participant must say what is bothering him or her without blowing the anger out of proportion. Feelings of displeasure must be channeled by thoughtful decisions for expressing oneself constructively. State why you are upset and how you disagree, and then stop. Do not seek to change or control your loved one through your anger. Trust that your argument will have an influence, and respect your partner enough to believe that he or she can handle the opinions you give.

Stay in the Middle of the Anger Channel

The reason for airing our disagreements in constructive arguments is to become closer to each other. We want to understand and be understood by others. Good anger expression must spring from a caring attitude toward the person with whom we are arguing. And caring requires a commitment to work through our differences. We are not to reject or write off those who spark our anger.

To direct anger into a positive course, we need to limit it and control it much like the banks of a river direct the flow of a river. One bank represents the extreme of not expressing any anger at all. The opposite bank represents the extreme of expressing anger violently and destructively. We must avoid the treacherous banks and seek the middle of the stream if we are to make unimpeded progress. We are responsible for our actions in expressing anger. We can decide to clam up or to act out. Or we can choose to be straightforward and clear with our anger, which will leave us feeling satisfied that we have had our say.

Jill: Catching Herself. Jill bided her time. She felt ignored by her husband, Lee, and didn't like it. She also noted on her secret score card that he wasn't very romantic.

Lee sat glued to the basketball game on TV, barely acknowledging Jill's presence. Finally the game was over, and he jubilantly exclaimed, "Boy, that was a great game! That final shot was a beauty—with just two seconds to go!" His voice faltered as he noticed the unhappy look on Jill's face.

"I'm upset with you, Lee," she began slowly. "You act like you don't care about me. When I talk to you, it's just like talking to a wall." Jill spoke rapidly and emotionally now. "You don't respond, you just say, 'uh-huh.' I need something better than that."

Lee, who listened with his mouth hanging open, leaned forward. "Now, just a minute," he interrupted angrily. "Here

I am having a good time watching my game and all of a sudden you jump on me. I feel like walking out the door when you come unglued like this. You need to tell me one thing at a time in a reasonable way and listen to what I say too."

Jill took a deep breath. She realized she had jumped on Lee because of her nervousness about confronting him. She consciously decided to control her emotions.

"I'm trying to say that I want you to pay more attention to me," she continued quietly. "Sometimes I feel left out, like you don't even notice me. I wish you'd sit down with me occasionally to talk about how we feel about things."

"I get the feeling that whatever I do it won't be right," Lee answered. "I get so frustrated that I don't even feel like trying."

Jill was aware of her tendency to panic in an angry confrontation. In this instance she was able to interrupt her usual pattern and control herself. Pausing for a deep breath helped her gain composure. It gave her time to think about how she was expressing herself.

Lee's pattern was to shut down when Jill overreacted. He panicked and stopped talking when he sensed the tempo of the conversation picking up. But in this example he decided to clearly state what he needed, and he was rewarded. When Jill slowed down, he was able to join in the conversation in a positive way. Both of them used their heads to express their angry feelings in a mature, constructive manner.

It is important to note that Lee and Jill are still expressing their emotions at the end of the conversation. They are not so controlled that the conversation became stoical or intellectual. It is possible and desirable to combine thoughts and feelings in a controlled yet emotionally charged argument.

Jill and Lee have learned to do this over a period of a few years. Now that they no longer harbor a hidden buildup of resentments, they are able to enjoy each other's company.

A Matter of Timing

There is a proper time and place for expressing anger. Since anger expression is a thoughtful decision as well as an emotional outburst, we need to choose the conditions most appropriate for expressing our feelings of displeasure. We need to ask ourselves several questions before speaking out. How well do I know this person? How much do I care about him or her? Who else is listening? Am I interrupting something more important? Would it be better to wait? How important is this confrontation to our relationship?

Time to Speak Out

We experience so many irritations with people every day that we cannot possibly confront them all. We must constantly evaluate which relationships are most deserving of our involved communication. Annoyances in the more important relationships are a priority. Something is out of balance if we spend ten minutes confronting the man at the dry cleaners about his poor workmanship but neglect expressing displeasure to our spouse about not having sex for two weeks.

We need to speak up as soon as possible after a disagreement. Prompt confrontation and resolution helps build positive relationships. Failure to speak up quickly allows resentments to build up, often resulting in a nonproductive explosion. At the earliest possible moment after the disagreement, express your displeasure in a simple, straightforward manner. Some simple, direct sentences that will work in most situations are:

"I don't agree with what you are saying."

"I think you are making this situation one-sided. I believe there are other ways of handling it."

"I would like to have the chance to tell you what I think."

"It bothers me that you interrupt me."

"I do not feel respected by you."

Jon and Chris: Withdrawal Patterns. When Jon and Chris came to me they were unwilling to express their anger to each other. They both came from families which did not express anger except on rare, explosive occasions. Jon and Chris, like their respective parents, had a pattern of withdrawing from each other when they felt angry or hurt. Sometimes they experienced weeks of silent loneliness.

As I worked with Jon and Chris, they realized that this pulling away kept them distant from each other. They came to appreciate the fresh start their relationship enjoyed after a good, clean argument. Here's an example of one:

As Chris finished doing the dishes, she glanced at Jon out of the corner of her eye. He seemed intent on his newspaper, but she wondered if he was feeling lonely and upset as she was. She realized she hadn't been feeling friendly with him and knew she must talk about it with him so she'd feel better. "Oh God," she prayed silently as she removed her apron, "help me find the right words to be close to Jon."

Chris sank into the comfortable chair beside Jon and asked, "Could we talk for a few minutes Jon, or are you right in the middle of something important?"

He looked up nervously and replied, "No, it's okay. I was just reading to unwind. What is it?"

She picked at her skirt hesitantly thinking, *I bet he'll blow up.* Then she looked him in the eye. "Jon, you don't seem very friendly lately, so I figure you're upset about me working. I'm angry you don't support me more."

Jon responded, "One of the reasons I'm not very friendly is because I feel you're leaving me out. Now that you're working, I feel like you're turning away from me. I'm angry that everything else seems more important to you than me."

"That's not true," Chris interrupted, leaning forward with her face flushing. "You are more important than any-thing else in my life. I miss you. I wish you weren't so prickly to approach."

There was a pause. Chris saw she had gotten through to him. He looked upset. Jon continued in a calmer voice. "I know I'm harsh sometimes, but you close up at times and you're not easy to approach either. I am glad you're working, Chris. I'm proud of you. But I get lonely, and I miss you too." He leaned over and hugged her.

Chris started out by being direct and to the point. She also expressed her feelings right away. Because Chris confronted Jon at a deep level, Jon was ready to respond at the same level. They were both willing to state their displeasure and tell each other they cared. Because of the involved, caring tone of the fight, Jon was willing to acknowledge his part in what was going wrong. This argument got Jon and Chris back on the right track of turning to each other instead of doing their own thing or creating more misunderstandings.

Time to Hold Back

There are times when it is better to postpone or forego altogether an angry confrontation. A mature, expressive person does not state displeasure immediately in every situation.Rather, there must be consideration for God's will and what is best for each person. Here are some examples:

You are with friends at a party when your spouse starts telling a story you've heard six times. Each time he embellishes the facts even more. You are irritated and want to say, "I don't like it that you tell the same canned stories over and over, especially when you exaggerate the truth." But you decide to express your displeasure later rather than embarrass him in front of your friends.

Your spouse is rushing to leave the house and frantically searching for her keys. She is creating an uproar and being unreasonably grouchy. Her childish behavior upsets you, but it's important that she makes her appointment on time. Later you confront her by saying, "I resent how grouchy you were this morning when you couldn't find your keys. I felt you were taking it out on me.

You arrive home to find your teenager sitting in front of the TV with a stack of dirty dishes on the kitchen counter.

You are instantly angry because you have worked hard all day and he has been loafing in front of the TV. But you decide not to jump on him immediately and create a defensiveness that cuts off all communication. So you say hello and share some comments about your day. Then you say, "I would like you to clean up your dishes. I get upset when I come home and find them on the counter."

You overhear your secretary making an appointment with a client at the front desk. You notice she is not as enthusiastic as you would like. You are tempted to move in on the conversation and take over, but this would be disrespectful to your secretary. Later you tell her, "I was disappointed that you sounded disinterested when you were making that appointment today. I want each person we see to feel important and special."

Let's Have a Good, Clean Fight

The method of anger expression we prescribe—staying within the boundaries of propriety—is a good, clean fight. We're not talking about physical battle. Nor are we talking about winning and losing. In this book, "fight" designates the thoughtful confrontation of disagreeing individuals for the purpose of expressing viewpoints.

Our anger varies in intensity according to the situation. Sometimes we merely exchange a few sentences expressing annoyance; at other times we trade sharp retorts. Perhaps we find ourselves both yelling at each other at the same time (we usually manage to hear the important points anyway).

In a good fight we must *focus* on what we need to express even while we are listening to what our partner tells us. Later, when the fighting has died down, our partner's words will sink in and have an effect. During the verbal exchange, however, listening too carefully to the other viewpoint will sap our strength. It weakens us to look at both sides equally at that time.

When two intimate persons become experienced fighters

and trust their anger fully, they will get to the root of their anger quickly. At the moment of conflict, veteran fighters will be able to state almost simultaneously the kernel of their disagreement. Their eyes flash, their bodies tense and their awareness of their surroundings fades. They exist together in an instant of deep emotional contact. A good, clean fight between two committed, caring people creates an emotional high. An exchange in which each partner is equally strong and hotly involved is a step toward closeness. We feel brave thinking of the warmth that will eventually follow.

When the fight is constructive, an observer can readily agree with both persons and see that the sharing is productive. Truthful statements are made by both participants. When the fight is over, there is a definite feeling of relief and the lightening of a heavy load. There is peace after the storm.

Of course, arguing is never easy and relaxed. Even when we know it's for the best, we feel upset when we fight. We want the other person to like us. Every time we disagree we risk rejection. But the increased understanding and passion is worth the discomfort!

We need to keep in mind that the more genuine we are, the better our relationship will be. As we fight we need to remind ourselves that the exchange will make us closer to each other. The angrier we are, the deeper our feelings will become for each other.

Learning the Ropes

Dan and Laurie: Strong, Caring Confrontation. Dan and Laurie are two strong and stubborn individuals. Both of them learned to be fiercely independent. Dan's mother died when he was seven years old, and his father withdrew to the extent that Dan felt like he was on his own. Laurie felt isolated from her family. She was embarrassed by her mother's messy housekeeping and her father's boisterous storytelling. At an early age she escaped into her own fantasy world in which she was the star.

Since both Dan and Laurie felt insecure and aloof, they tended to build up unexpressed resentments in their relationship until they exploded. With counseling they learned how to fight well and often, and their arguments no longer felt like the end of the world.

I remember a group session when Dan arrived with a clear purpose in mind: It was time for him to clear the air with Laurie. She had been picking on Dan for a day or two, and he had withdrawn into his garage with his tools.

As soon as the fight started, Dan and Laurie participated fully. They both raised their voices at the same time, yet their manner was respectful. They were totally engrossed in what they were saying, and their words tumbled out spontaneously. They were each concentrating on their own resentments, though it was plain that they were also listening to each other.

Dan was angry with Laurie for being demanding and selfish and for leaving him out of her plans. When their friends came around he felt overlooked. Group members were cheering Dan on by agreeing with his points.

Laurie was angry with Dan for joking around instead of seriously telling her how he felt. She resented his moodiness and quietness, and she often felt frustrated that he would only share with her when he was ready. We cheered her on by agreeing with her points.

As they talked, they built on each other's comments and acknowledged each other's position.

"Laurie, I'm mad because you didn't ask me before inviting your mother and father for the weekend," Dan said. "I don't feel you're respecting me when you don't check with me before inviting them over!"

"If I asked you, you'd hem and haw and put me off," Laurie replied. "The feeling I get is that if you had your way, we'd never have anyone over."

"That's not true, though I'd probably do it less than you want to," he answered. "I want you to consider my needs. I don't feel special."

Laurie paused and considered what she had just heard. She said more slowly, "You are special. I think I was afraid you'd say 'no' if I asked you about my parents' visit. I want to see them very much. I know you don't enjoy them sometimes, and that hurts me. I wish you'd put yourself out more for them."

The more Laurie talked, the more Dan softened and opened up to her. "I like your parents," he said, "though sometimes we don't get along. I didn't realize you have been missing them recently. I wish you'd just say that."

When the fight ended they both looked animated and energetic. Clearly, they trusted the foundation of their relationship. Neither of them felt rejected or nervous about later repercussions. They said what they needed to say and they were done with it, and they were ready to let the feelings sink in.

Dan and Laurie were able to sift through what they heard each other say. Since they respected each other's opinions, each could see the truth in what the other said. And they could feel each other's loneliness. As they did so, they began to feel some hurt. Expressing the hurt softened them and made them vulnerable to each other. By the end of the group session they were ready to go home and be close. It was exciting to see them go from isolation to closeness in such a short span of time.

Dan and Laurie now have the tools they need for closeness. Their only stumbling block is the fear they feel before they start a fight. They are certainly successful at the actual process of fighting, and gradually they have developed the confidence they need to "keep at it" regularly at home. They have improved to the point where they flow from anger to hurt to warmth within a few hours. No more wasted days and weeks of built-up feelings for them!

Let the Feelings Sink In

The good expression of anger between two people is moving and dignified for them and to observers. Once the main statements are made, usually a silence falls and the fight is over. Nothing remains to be said; anything more would be anticlimactic.

At this point fighting partners need to back off and let the feelings sink in. It's okay to be around each other while mulling over the argument in thoughtful silence. Partners might fix dinner together, continue to get dressed to go out or talk casually to each other or the children. Depending upon the depth of the anger, they may choose to be quiet with their thoughts for a few minutes or a few hours.

On a deeper level, the hurt is settling in and there may be sadness, frustration, loneliness and vulnerability. In this valuable time we learn about ourselves. The hurt causes us to take a more honest look at what we are doing to contribute to the problem. Later it is good to share these feelings with each other. If we are honest when we humbly say what we have done wrong, we will understand each other better and feel a surge of warmth. Certainly, times of hurt and vulnerability can be among the closest for a couple. In good fighting each partner begins to see the other's viewpoint, making it possible to cry on each other's shoulder. Crying together is a sharing that bonds two into one, just as God wants for us. Crying together says, "I trust you completely in this moment."

Then comes the warmth! The sun comes out, and the depth of anger and hurt is reflected in the depth of the love that is felt. Experiencing all three of these basic feelings with a loved one makes us truly glad to be alive and together.

In this chapter we have talked about the boundaries of healthy anger expression. Next we need to discover specific methods for anger expression which will help us achieve our goals of closeness.

Chapter Three

Let Your Anger Out

"You have heard that it was said to the people long ago , 'Do not murder, and anyone who murders will be subject to judgment.' But I tell you that anyone who is angry with his brother will be subject to judgment. Again, anyone who says to his brother, 'Raca,' is answerable to the Sanhedrin. But anyone who says, 'You fool!' will be in danger of the fire of hell."

Matthew 5:21-22

We will be judged by God for our anger unless it is expressed in positive, constructive ways. Each time we are openly angry we are accountable to God. I know that Jesus is listening in when I speak angry words. I think to myself how it must sound to him, and that helps me to do a good job. There are right ways and wrong ways to communicate our feelings of displeasure in our relationships.

In this chapter we will identify several wrong approaches to anger expression we must avoid. Then we will describe a number of right ways to share our anger with others.

Anger Going the Wrong Way

Anger has a bad reputation among Christians because it is often wrongly expressed. For centuries people have been taught one of the deadly sins is anger, and its opposite virtue is humility. But remember: Anger is a feeling, and feelings are neither right nor wrong. Of course, our behavioral responses to our feelings can be—and often are—wrong. Three fighting styles to avoid when expressing anger are overreacting (domineering), withholding (hinting) and indirectness (sarcasm).

Nobody Likes a Bully

Rod and Hazel: Domineering Anger. Hazel sat in the living room talking nonstop to her husband, Rod, about her day, her life and their family. Rod responded with an occasional grunt. Suddenly Hazel stopped. "Rod, you never tell me how you're feeling, and I'm sick of it. Here I am sharing with you, and you're not willing to say anything."

"That's not true," Rod responded. "It's difficult for me to talk to you because you don't even stop to take a breath."

"You had some big problems in your family while you were growing up," she continued, as though he hadn't spoken, "and if you don't start working on some of that I never will get close to you."

"I feel close to you," he said with a shrug of his shoulders. "After all, we've raised three children and we've been together for 15 years."

"It takes more than that to be close," she replied with a stab of anger.

After a pause, Rod turned away. "You don't know what you're talking about," he said disparagingly.

Hazel defeated her attempt at closeness by bombarding Rod with negative statements. The use of the word "never" (or other absolutes) is exaggerated and closes down any meaningful discussion. When people are told they "never" or "always" do something they feel so discouraged they want to give up. Hazel lorded herself over Rod by analyzing and threatening him.

Rod defended himself in a pleading manner, and she squelched him with her last statement, which implied that he did not have what it took to be close. Rod never got into the conversation for himself. Instead he reacted defensively to Hazel's comments and tried hard to please her. In the end he felt she had no respect and thus retaliated by discrediting everything Hazel said.

Anger which dominates through negativism and attack is nonproductive. It is one-sided and judgmental, and it works against closeness.

Withholding Anger Pushes Others Away

Rod and Hazel: Pushing the Wrong Buttons. When Hazel wasn't domineering Rod with her anger, she often tried to accomplish her ends through hints and innuendos.

One morning Hazel and Rod were getting showered and dressed. Hazel wanted to ask Rod to come to her softball team's party but was too intimidated to ask him straightforwardly. Instead she said, "I'm going to a party for the softball team on Saturday night, and most of the husbands will be there."

"I'm working on Saturday, and I'll be tired by the end of the day," Rod answered. "By Saturday night I'll just want to relax and watch TV."

"I thought you were going to start taking a half day off on Saturdays," Hazel pressed critically.

"Saturday is an important day for big sales," Rod answered defensively, "and *someone* has to work hard around here to earn the money for the family."

"Don't rub it in," Hazel sighed with exasperation. "Anyway, I'll go by myself as usual, and I won't be out late."

"I'll probably be asleep by the time you get home, so don't hurry," he said.

In this exchange, Hazel and Rod completely missed communicating. Did Hazel want Rod to come with her? Did Rod feel slighted that he was not asked? Did Hazel resent that Rod worked hard at the expense of fun? Did Rod feel insulted that he was accused of being no fun? Hazel tried to use guilt to manipulate Rod into attending the party. But they missed connecting with each other in this conversation.

Instead of using guilt as a crow-bar to pry Rod loose from his Saturday schedule, Hazel might have done better to approach him honestly: "Rod, I like being with you. On Saturday my softball team is having a party. I'd like you to come to the party. Will you come with me?"

"I'm working on Saturday," Rod replies, "but maybe I could leave a little early. You know I don't like going to parties very much. But I'll try to come because it's important to you."

"It is important to me," she continues. "I'll stay with you so you'll feel more comfortable. The main thing I like is to have you there with me."

Rod and Hazel eventually did learn to talk directly. They felt awkward at first and made mistakes, but both of them persevered and mastered the necessary skills one by one. They succeeded because they loved each other and wanted a better relationship. They truly meant the commitment they had made to stay married until death would part them.

Avoid Indirectness

Another common way people express anger wrongly is through the indirectness of sarcasm. Sarcasm is communication marked by caustic, cutting remarks. Sarcastic expressions of anger create confusion and raise barriers between partners.

Roy and Linda: Hiding Behind Sarcasm. When Roy and Linda first came to see me, they avoided conversation about important issues. Linda was more verbal than Roy, and she wanted Roy to talk to her more. She wanted him to take more responsibility around the house and for their child.

Roy acted weak and seemed immature about being a husband and father. Early in their therapy he was almost silent. In a martyr's voice, Linda recited a long list of complaints. She had an iron-clad case against Roy, but she was not expressing her feelings as she told the story.

Roy smiled, squirmed in his chair and occasionally made a small protest or asked Linda to explain something. I pushed him to react to Linda's charges. Some of his comments were: "She's the one who understands feelings, not me."

"I gave that over to Linda long ago because she knows so much more about that than I do."

"Why don't you ask Linda?"

"If you say so, then it must be right."

On the surface his responses were acceptable. Still there was a sarcastic edge to his voice and a flicker of hostility in his eye. He was seething with anger, but he was expressing it with subtle but biting sarcasm.

When I confronted his sarcasm, Roy flashed a wide-eyed look of innocence and insisted that he really meant what he said. But after a dozen confrontations his guard began to slip, and some direct anger began to emerge. When Roy's anger came out more directly, Linda, who had played the role of the martyr, began to fight back. Suddenly there was sarcasm in *her* voice as she directed her responses to Roy:

"I know it's hard for you, but I'd like you to get home one night a week when you say you're going to."

"I'm sorry to ask so much of you, but you've been saying for five months that you would reseed the lawn."

"I would appreciate it if you would keep me company instead of falling asleep on the couch in front of the TV."

I pointed out that they were both being sarcastic. As counseling usually reveals, both husband and wife were contributing equally to the problem. Often one partner appears to be in the right while the other seems wrong, but if we look closer we see that both play their part. Like children on a see-saw, Roy and Linda took turns putting themselves up and the other one down. Their poor expression of anger sabotaged closeness.

I confronted them. "You are both causing the problems

you are having," I said. "I see you being competitive and disrespectful to each other. I want you to talk to each other from the heart, saying exactly what you mean." They responded well to my statements. They seemed relieved and humbled.

Much of the subterfuge fell away and some good, direct arguing began to occur. Gradually their relationship became more balanced and the exchanges more equal in strength. Underneath, their intentions were good. They both wanted the best for their family. Much of the competitiveness disappeared. They became interested in expressing their displeasure directly and dealing with it openly. After they stopped tearing each other down through sarcasm they were able to build each other up through constructive, direct anger expression.

Accentuate Positive Anger

In contrast to negative, nonproductive expressions of anger, there are several positive, productive ways to communicate our feelings of displeasure in relationships.

Tell The Truth

The truth, simply stated from the heart, is the best means of gaining closeness. While we need to be careful to not be abusive or attacking, it is important to speak as freely as possible when we're angry without over-censoring our comments. We need to trust ourselves more and risk the hurt of rejection. Hurt is not bad, and nine times out of ten you will not be rejected!

The other person must also have a chance to respond so that there will be an exchange. We must talk back and forth until the "shadow" disappears. Then we feel understood. The joys will outweigh the sorrows when we speak up and when we listen closely to the other person's point of view. When we are willing to stick our necks out about how we feel, we are more likely to be acknowledged. And even if our needs are not met, we will feel strong and not regret we have shared our feelings.

To fully express our feelings we must not censor our words unduly. Keeping in mind our caring for the other person, we need the freedom to explore new territories. If we say something regrettable, we can admit it. When we are overly controlled in an argument we pick and chose our words too carefully. We pussyfoot around the other person to the point of losing our effectiveness. Our message is muffled by the padded words we use to soften each other's anger. Our true meaning is not expressed, and the opportunity to have a constructive fight is lost.

Our intellect must remain *in charge* of our feelings at all times. Within that framework we can be spontaneous in our fighting and allow our words to come tumbling out. Other important filters for our anger are a mutual respect for one another and a position of nonviolence toward each other. Once we have decided to keep our minds in charge and to stay respectful and nonviolent, we can relax and be our spontaneous selves in the argument.

Bob and Sally: Spilling the Beans. Bob was annoyed that Sally was in a bad mood. "I don't like your grouchiness tonight. I'm disappointed that you put so much of yourself into your work that I don't get enough good time with you," he complained.

"I wish you'd just tell me that you understand I worked hard today and that you appreciate me," Sally replied. "Then I'd feel better. I hate your being so critical of me. I am tired, and I don't want you to tell me it's all my fault. I am working on controlling my schedule, but I'm having a hard time saying no to commitments."

"I guess I'm not sure that I can make a difference," Bob responded. "Sometimes I don't think my opinion matters to you. I think you'll just work harder anyway. But it's good to know that my being warm could help you feel better."

"Your opinion matters to me!" Sally exclaimed enthusiastically. "And your hugs and warm words can turn my mood around." Then they hugged each other.

Sally and Bob said just what they thought and felt, and it worked. They attracted warmth by being vulnerable. They were enthused about how well this worked. The more they talked spontaneously the better they liked it and the easier it became. They enjoyed knowing what was going on rather than guessing.

Spontaneous argument gives us greater insight into what is really happening. We hear what is bothering each other. We allow each other to see how much we truly care. Being vulnerable makes closeness possible.

The following statements are examples of straightforward expressions of anger that cut through the games and avoidance in relationships:

"I feel unhappy tonight because you're not giving me your attention."

"I want to feel special to you. I wish you were more excited to be with me."

"I'm angry that you interrupt me when I'm talking. I don't feel respected."

"I want your support. I'm upset that you don't listen to what's important to me."

"I'm upset that you didn't include me in your final decision. I want my opinion to be important to you."

Be Appropriate to the Relationship Level

We need to reserve our most expressive anger for the people we love the most. We should be most angry with the people with whom we are intimate, and only annoyed with strangers. Anger requires energy. If someone matters to us they are able to get our goat. The more love we feel for someone the more angry we become when they do something we don't like.

Unfortunately, we often are overwhelmed by fear of anger in our intimate relationships. We are tempted to let off steam in relationships which are unimportant to us. Sometimes we take our problems with our spouses out on our coworkers. We must learn to express our anger at the appropriate level for the depth of our relationship. For example, at work we may express that we are annoyed, in a friendship that we are angry, and in a close relationship that we are furious (one step below rage).

Anger on the Job

Joy and Skip: A Business Discussion. Joy has been working for Skip for a year. During a staff meeting Skip asked her opinion of his management skills. She needed to think carefully about how much to say and how strongly to speak based on clues from past interactions with him.

"I'm glad you're my boss," Joy stated immediately. Then she thoughtfully continued. "But sometimes you seem preoccupied, and I feel strictly on my own with my work. I could use more feedback on how I'm doing. And sometimes you leave too much up to me. I'd like stronger direction from you."

"I'm still learning about being a boss," Skip confessed. "I'm open to your suggestions. I'm also willing to spend more time talking about plans, but I still want you to act independently."

"You've been doing this work for years," Joy continued, "so I need the benefit of your experience. And yes, I like being independent and feeling trusted."

Since her boss was open to her feedback, Joy was free to express herself. But she was careful not to go too far. She picked one important item to discuss and gave positive comments along with the negative. It was important she began by saying, "I'm glad you are my boss." That laid the foundation so that everything that followed would be constructive.

It is not appropriate to be deeply emotional at work. We reserve that level of caring for our personal relationships. Sometimes we are in close relationships with the people at work, but we should express those feelings outside of the office. It is appropriate to say "I am upset today," but not to cry hysterically or go on and on about a problem we have. We need to let people at work know when we are having a bad day so they can help, but the work must continue.

Anger between Friends

Dianne and Liz: Dinner Disagreement. Dianne invited her friend Liz to a dinner party at her house. Liz said she would try to attend but did not arrive or even call. The next day the following conversation took place on the telephone:

"I was upset that you didn't come to my party or even call," Dianne said. "It seemed that my party wasn't important to you."

"I did tell you that I probably couldn't come because of my work schedule. I really wanted to come," responded Liz.

"I would have appreciated a final call to make your plans clear. I wasn't sure how many people to plan for," said Dianne.

"I agree," said Liz, "I should have called. Actually I should have said 'no' when you first asked me, but I didn't want to hurt your feelings."

Dianne and Liz expressed their displeasure on an appropriate level. Because they were new friends they were not deeply upset about their disagreement. By talking it through they strengthened their relationship. They realized that neither of them had taken the invitation lightly.

Disagreements in Intimate Relationships

Dianne and Trent: Intimate Disagreement. Dianne expressed herself more deeply with Trent, the man she had been dating for a year. Gradually they had been finding out about each other. They had shared about their family, growing up years and previous relationships. Now they were learning to say how they felt in present situations. Dianne and Trent had just finished dinner together when Dianne decided to bring up an issue that had been bothering her.

"I'm angry that you have planned your vacation without considering me," she began. "I would like to do something with you at least part of the time."

"I'm angry too," Trent replied. "You plan your trips without a thought for me. The last time you went to Laguna, I called you, and you almost bit my head off. You are so unfriendly sometimes."

"When you phoned me, you didn't sound friendly," she continued. "I get so frustrated. Are you paying me back for not sharing my vacation with you?"

"Maybe," Trent responded thoughtfully. "I need more encouragement from you. Sometimes I don't feel you're caring for me. I didn't know until now that you wanted to do something with me on this vacation."

Both Dianne and Trent made themselves vulnerable in this exchange. Rather than continuing to go their separate ways by acting unconcerned, they clearly asked for more caring from each other. They took big risks because they wanted a deeper relationship. Now they could stop playing cat and mouse and plan a vacation together.

Use Appropriate Intensity

The depth of our expressed feelings needs to match the closeness of our relationship. The deeper our feelings are for a person (or a cause, for that matter), the deeper our anger will be. The intensity of our anger will later be matched by the intensity of our hurt and warmth.

Hate is ugly. It is too intense. It generally begins with feeling angry toward a person we care about. We hold our anger until it grows out of proportion. Our good feelings are buried under a pile of resentments. We need to get to the bottom of our resentments for our anger to be a positive experience rather than a bad one. It is normal and healthy to feel strong emotion. Yet we all recognize times when we let our negative feelings take over.

It is important not to allow the shifting sands of our emotions to be mixed with cement and become hardened. We need to be flexible with our feelings. One moment we feel intensely angry with someone. Moments later the feeling can turn to hurt.Later it can turn to warmth. We need to trust our feelings to flow so they do not become bottled up.

The Necessary Sights and Sounds of Anger

We need to let anger come and go naturally like the ebb and flow of the waves on the sand. Between the extremes of being silent and exploding we have a lot of room for expressing anger. We need to practice proper anger expression and count on our intellects to guide us at critical moments. Our heads can and should rule our feelings so we will be effective. We must be careful not to become proud of being easily angered. If we are comfortable with our anger we don't feel the need to get the jump on anyone. We need only to make clear statements and listen to the feedback we get from those who witness our anger. We need to show anger and then drop it. No fuming and rerunning it in our minds for hours. We said it, they heard it, that's enough!

If we think anger is bad, often we go to great lengths to tone down our expression of anger. However, we should look and sound angry when we are. We should loosen up and trust ourselves not to go too far. The truth will set us free. As long as we don't go overboard, we can say honestly how we feel. Some sparkle in our eyes adds zest to our personalities and our lives.

Let's face it, our feelings are, by definition, irrational. To truly experience that surge of adrenaline which our anger excites, we must be spontaneous. It is important to give ourselves the freedom of feeling riled up. When we let ourselves feel angry, we know we are alive. We feel excited, energetic and fully involved in the present moment. Our intellect stands ready to intervene appropriately to stop any violence.

Why are we so afraid to show we are angry? We may think that if we allow ourselves to express any anger we will rage out of control and hurt someone. Actually the reverse is true. If we allow ourselves an outlet for our anger, we are able to feel good about ourselves. But if we let unexpressed anger build up, we will eventually explode. When that happens, our anger comes out in destructive ways that leave us feeling awful about ourselves.

It's Okay to Raise Your Voice

Many of us like to express our differences of opinion in a calm, reasonable tone of voice. In our intimate relationships, however, we sometimes need to get excited and even shout to strongly release our anger. With practice we can express many disagreements in simple, straightforward sentences, raising our voices as necessary. If we allow ourselves to yell occasionally, to let off our angry steam, we will never reach the point of lashing out in violent behavior. Even when we shout we can be respectful in our words, tone of voice and manner. In my own marriage, for example, if we are expressing anger well, Jack and I may disagree daily for a few minutes, be angry twice a week for five minutes and yell once a month.

Hazel and Rod: Loud Exchange. Hazel and Rod were steaming with anger because the issue over which they were arguing was important and had come up many times in one form or another. They both found the situation upsetting, and they were both able to say what they needed to—in angry, raised voices—without losing respect for each other or themselves.

Hazel had been arguing with their 25-year-old daughter, Barbara, during the day. Barbara had avoided looking for a job as she had promised, and she left the kitchen in a mess even after Hazel requested that Barbara clean up after herself.

Hazel dreaded approaching Rod for support because he had been taking Barbara's side. Yet this time she felt strongly that the situation needed to improve. She waited until they were alone in the evening and said strongly, "Rod, I had a terrible day with Barbara. She's been lying around the house not doing anything. It's painful to watch her and know she's not feeling good about herself."

"She'll be okay," Rod answered. "I know she'll do what she needs to when she's ready. Picking on her only makes matters worse."

"Rod, it's time for Barbara to move out of our house," Hazel said with her voice rising in volume. "She's 25 years old, and it's not helping her to live with us. If she had to take care of herself, I think she'd get on with her life."

"No way," Rod retorted loudly and angrily. "She needs our help and support. There's no way I'm going to put her out. I like having her here."

"You are so rejecting," Hazel shouted. "I don't even feel you are listening to me. You prefer Barb to me. I'd like to be alone with you for a change."

Rod shouted back, "Threatening Barb is no way to get close to me. You just go around looking for trouble. Why don't you leave things the way they are?"

"The way they are is not good," she said, matching his angry tone."I want you to open your eyes."

Each walked away to calm down and think over what had been said. The issue of asking their daughter to leave their home was serious and traumatic for both Rod and Hazel. It was understandable they would feel threatened and deserted by each other's disagreement. But here they were both able to let off some steam and thus feel more of the underlying hurt which was needed to soften their positions. Later they were able to have a more reasonable discussion. After several more exchanges they were able to come up with a plan they could both agree upon.

God wants the husband and wife to be a team when they raise their children. Disagreements must be ironed out no matter how painful it is to discuss them. It may take many talks, some heated, before resolution takes place. In the end your children will feel secure that Mom and Dad are together.

Keep Your Ears Open

Though our main focus is on what we need to say, secondarily we need to be sure to listen during a disagreement. Remember that a good fight is an *exchange* of information. When we fight, both of us have good points to make. We need to be careful not to get so defensive that our partner's words roll off us. We must decide in advance to respectfully hear what our partner says. If the argument is heated, we may both raise our voices, and sometimes we will be talking at the same time. Even then it is possible to hear the important points that are said.

In a positive, intimate relationship the words shouted at us in anger should not be heard as rejection. Rather, we are being given information that will help us to get closer. I often tell myself, "This is only a fight; this will blow over. Listen to the message." I also remind myself that this person must care a lot about me to be so angry with me. The criticism we hear will help us to see ourselves more clearly. We are forced to look at the parts of ourselves we might normally avoid. This is painful, but we are more lovable to each other if we admit our flaws.

It is helpful for us to acknowledge our partner's position in the argument. In order to be a good combatant, we need to swallow our pride and give our partner credit for his or her insights. We don't need to agree, but we should respond with a statement of acknowledgment such as:

"Okay, I hear you."

"I'll think about what you've said."

"You've made your point; that's enough."

In the following example Tom and Jean learned from listening to each other when they argued. In their argument, one point built upon another. They had not made up their minds in advance of their arguing and were willing to be influenced by the interaction.

Tom and Jean: Listening and Advancing. Jean had gone back to school to finish earning her B.A. degree. Tom was upset with her for procrastinating on her studying.

"When you tell me what to do, Tom, I want to do just the opposite," Jean began. "You're too bossy! You're not my father."

"I think you like me taking care of you," Tom answered, "like when you get behind on studying, and you want me to grocery shop and fix dinner. I resent that."

"Nobody makes you do anything," she said. "If you don't like it, then don't help me. I resent your ordering me around."

"I feel like I have to hold things together," Tom added. "If there's no food, what are we going to eat? I can't afford to have problems of my own when you have one crisis after another."

"I didn't know you felt that way, Tom! You usually seem to have everything under control, so I don't even feel needed. What's bothering *you*? I'm interested in hearing your problems."

In this conversation, Tom and Jean have given each other important information. They have opened up new possibilities on better ways of relating to each other. Jean may decide to be less helpless. Tom may decide to be less controlling. They are open to learning from each other. This is good listening.

Of course, one conversation didn't solve their problem, but it was a start in the right direction. Change happens best in little steps. That way neither person feels they've had to compromise. Subtly they influence each other so the result evolves without effort. This requires trusting God, each other and the process of good communication.

Go for Long-Term Gains

When we argue we need to look toward long-term gains rather than immediate results. We may need to have many discussions before we feel satisfied. Pushing our will on others will not work! They will push back, we will feel rejected and our ideas won't be taken seriously. We need to relax, repeat our opinions whenever necessary (without trying to change the other person) and let resolution emerge gradually.

Plant Seeds

Often the same issue will come up over and over again, but the fight/discussion is never the same. Each time we plant the seeds of our own position, and some seeds from both sides will sprout. Since we respect each other, we have a strong effect. The words we say will matter. Unconsciously we mull over the ideas expressed in the argument, and each of us slightly modifies his or her stand. Each is powerful in what is said, though most of us don't feel that way initially. We will notice the aftereffects weeks or months later. We can't expect instant results as though we're putting coins in a candy machine.

Mark and Betsy: Moving Forward through Repetition. Mark and Betsy had been fighting for years about being late whenever they went places together. Gradually they rubbed off on each other so that being late is no longer such a heavy issue between them. But their solution was the result of a long-running period of interchanges like the following:

"Mark, I'm really angry that you decided to take a shower now when we're suppose to be leaving," Betsy complained. "I hate being late, and we're taking some of the appetizers."

"I'll be ready before you are, Betsy," Mark snapped back. "You complain, but when I go to the car you're never there waiting."

"I just keep busy until you're ready to walk out so I don't get upset," she said.

"The last two times you were on the phone when I went out the door," answered Mark. "I think you want to make being late all my fault. Besides, I wish you'd relax about the time. I watch the clock all week. I don't want to punch a time clock when we go out for fun."

Until Betsy stated her resentment openly, she was 100 percent convinced their lateness was all Mark's fault. After a number of exchanges, she became aware that she *did* dawdle and that she couldn't lay the entire blame on him. From the arguing, Mark recognized his unrealistic expectations of what he could accomplish in the time allotted. He saw that he was dragging his feet because Betsy pushed him. Each time they fought, the argument was slightly different. New ideas came across or old ideas sank in. Growth, to be genuine and lasting, needs to be slow. Keep going; don't give up. Patience and endurance shows a deep level of commitment.

Look for Growth, Not Change.

It is important that two persons fight to share, learn and grow closer together—not to change each other. We are all unique and special, the product of God's creation, our genes and environment. If we tend to be quiet and gentle we will remain basically that type of person, though we can learn to be more talkative and forceful at times. If we are outgoing and aggressive we will always be that kind of person, though we can learn to be better listeners and to be vulnerable at times.

Asking another person to change implies that he or she is inferior or bad. Each of us needs to be accepted for who we are. It is good we are different from each other—it makes our lives much more interesting and broadens our perspectives. We all bring our own gifts to life, and we should be respected for that. Acceptance, rather than agitating for change, should characterize our relationships and disagreements. Only God has the right to demand change, and he has made that possible through his Son, Jesus. After we accept Christ, it is up to us to grow in the Spirit.

My husband and I are two different personality types. I am an outgoing person, full of words and feelings. He is a visual, physical person who likes to ponder before replying. I'm embarrassed to admit that for years I was certain my style of relating was the right one. And I wanted him to adopt it! He felt badly because I was so disappointed in him. He also felt unappreciated and angry with me. Fortunately, with feedback I realized God loves Jack as much as me. I gained a new respect for Jack and continue to learn from him daily.

Larry and Anna: Finding Balance. Anna is a shy, quiet, reserved person. She found herself attracted to Larry, who is gregarious, dominant and sometimes aggressive. He liked her gentleness, and she admired his confidence. Rather than changing each other, they learned from each other and found a balance together.

"I enjoy being with you," Anna said. "But I would like you to tell me what you don't like, instead of babying me."

"I know you're very sensitive," Larry replied. "I like to help you and protect you. It's easier for me to handle some situations that make you uncomfortable. I am a big talker compared to you."

"I am learning to talk more, and I need you to listen," Anna persevered. "I'd like to hear your opinion, but don't take me by the hand and do everything for me—like arranging a job for me."

"I know I sometimes take over," he commented sheepishly. "Point it out to me when I do, and I'll listen. I do like to hear what you've got to say. I wish you'd get after some job interviews."

"I know I need to be more assertive. I'll probably never

be as quick to act as you. But I want you to give me time and not be impatient with me," Anna replied.

"That's okay," he said. "We are different, and I'm glad we are. Two of me would be too much."

The differences between these two people helped them grow together rather than drift apart. Anna learned to be more assertive, while Larry learned patience. Actually, we usually are attracted to and select someone different from ourselves for intimate relationships. Partners who focus on mutual growth instead of change can combine their abilities and strengths to expand their respective and combined boundaries.

It's important that we not be competitive. Imagine that the two of you are in a canoe on a rough lake. You each have a paddle and need to work together in rhythm so that you don't capsize. If you stop paddling and start hitting each other over the head with the paddles, you will be in big trouble.

Arguing will help us get closer, but only if we do it well. We have discussed good ways to argue, and these strategies will take practice in the face of mistakes and discouragement. But with patience good, constructive fighting will become second nature to us.

Chapter Four

Conquer Your Fear of Anger

"There is no fear in love. But perfect love drives
out fear, because fear has to do with punishment. The
man who fears is not made perfect in love."
1 John 4:18

God offers us perfect love. If we trust him fully we can
let go, and he will catch us. We don't need to struggle so
hard or be anxious in the situations that occur in our lives.
He will not give us more than we can handle. *His* plan for
us is much better than any we could invent. But since we
know God's perfect plan includes loving one another and
becoming one with our spouses, why are we so fearful to
open our mouths?

The previous chapters offer evidence that positive anger
expression is good and necessary in the process of developing closeness in intimate relationships. True, we must carefully and strictly avoid wrong ways to express anger. But we
have studied many constructive methods for anger expression which can help build intimacy between spouses, friends
and co-workers. The pluses far outweigh the minuses: positive anger expression is a healthy and helpful interpersonal
endeavor.

But if anger expression is beneficial, why are we so

hesitant to practice it in our close relationships? What are the reasons we do not express anger as we should? Our heads may accept the evidence of anger's value in relationships, but at the first sign of disagreement with someone our hearts often rebel. We may *know* that anger expression is good and necessary, but we often don't *feel* like it's the right thing for us to do.

I have seen fear cause many people to panic and do strange things. A client changed her appointment six times in one week yet claimed she wasn't afraid of anything. A husband got drunk instead of facing a counseling session with his wife. A young man took his own life rather than face his parents to admit he had been dealing drugs. What stops us from expressing anger?

Personal fear keeps us from following through with anger expression. We have not learned to trust God and our own anger. We have not had enough practice with our anger to have confidence that we can handle it properly. We all have mishandled our anger before, and we're afraid that because we don't fully understand our anger we will mishandle it again.

Fear of being labeled a bad, angry person keeps us from doing what we should. We weren't trained to be constructively angry so we have no skills to fall back on. No wonder we feel shaky. We need guidelines. We were taught math, English, science and history but we never had a course in expressing feelings or in developing a good relationship. I wish we had a chance to learn these things in the first grade.

We think to ourselves, "If I do this wrong I may be rejected." We all fear rejection to some extent. Because we want everyone to like us, we are tempted to settle for keeping relationships tranquil rather than risking the disruption of an angry confrontation.

Our bottom line may be that we think we are not acceptable. We fear anger will expose us as inferior. One client told me, "I don't mind the hurt of being with someone I love who is sick, dying or suffering in some way—as long as I didn't cause it. What I can't stand is someone being angry *with me.* I hate rejection." Agreement for the sake of peace may gain us the approval we seek, but temporary approval is shallow compared to genuine, candid love.

Inappropriate patterns for handling anger from our original families often leave us fearful of expressing it. As young children we were wrongly programmed to fear and avoid anger. Bart witnessed his dad shoving his mother against the wall and swearing at her. Joan remembers, with a shudder, her mother throwing water in her dad's face. Matt recalls his dad slamming the door and leaving for hours. Susan endured her mom and dad sitting at the dinner table in tense silence. Barbara woke up in the middle of the night to loud fighting between her parents. No one explained to these children what was going on or reassured them the outcome would be good. As a matter of fact, the results of these forms of anger expression were usually destructive.

Our important role models—parents, other adults in our families, teachers, coaches, scout leaders—were often upset by our angry outbursts. Our experiences with childish anger in an adult world were mostly negative. Since most adults are uncertain about anger expression themselves they are uncomfortable with angry children. Rather than teaching the right way to be angry they try to turn the anger off. This sin has been passed on from generation to generation. The adults in our lives did not like us when we were angry and punished us accordingly.

Therefore, we need to reevaluate our original family patterns for dealing with anger. Some of these patterns may not be effective for us now, and we may want to deliberately choose new attitudes and ways of expressing ourselves. As dependent children we needed to adapt to survive. We did not have power to make changes then. However, as adults we can face anger with strength.

In my childhood home family members responded to

unpleasant topics by changing the subject and avoiding confrontation. One day my mother and aunt started to disagree about the care of Grandma. My sister, who had been trained to defuse arguments, said, "Look how beautiful the blue sky is." It didn't fit into the context of the conversation, but it was a signal to stop disagreeing. And it worked.

I was always disappointed when the arguments were cut off. Our family had a lot of uncompleted issues. After a period of leaving sensitive topics undiscussed, there would be occasional explosions. For example, my dad would blow up about my mom's bills from the department store. He would rant and rave for awhile. My mom would back off in the face of Dad's overreacting and wait it out. Even as a kid I was puzzled. I sensed something more important needed to be said, but it wasn't stated.

As an adult I have been able to change this unsuccessful pattern, choosing instead to foster an atmosphere of consistent openness and confrontation with my husband and children. It's been a gradual process of pushing through my fear to bravely speak up.

To Fear or Not to Fear?

We are designed by God to live good, productive lives full of joy with the people around us. Paul wrote: "For we are God's workmanship, created in Christ Jesus to do good works, which God prepared in advance for us to do" (Ephesians 2:10). Later Paul clarified that the positive relationship we enjoy with others is to be surrounded by love: ". . . and live a life of love, just as Christ loved us and gave himself up for us as a fragrant offering and sacrifice to God." (Ephesians 5:2).

Loving relationships with others leading to mutually productive lives is what God has in mind for us. But we humans are encumbered with annoying frailties that create barriers that keep us apart from each other. As 1 John 4:18 suggests, fear is at the root of the barriers which prevent us from loving each other as we should. We are afraid to trust our own feelings. We are afraid to trust other people. We are afraid that if we express our anger we will upset the delicate balance of the relationship, and it will fall apart.

We all experience fear, and some fears are good. Healthy fear is necessary to physical and emotional well-being. We need to be afraid of some situations which are potentially dangerous to our health, like riding a bicycle in heavy traffic. We also need to be afraid of certain people with unsound values who try to take advantage of us, like someone who encourages us to try cocaine.

Some fear is necessary to produce the adrenaline we need if we are to do the best possible job, whether riding our bike safely, speaking in front of an audience or expressing our feelings to a loved one. But too much fear will defeat us or cause us to blank out and forget what we are saying. Too much fear weakens us so we lose confidence and feel insecure.

Probably seventy-five percent of our fear is unnecessary. Feelings will not do us in. On the contrary, the *absence* of feelings or panicking because of our feelings *might* kill us. We must remember that God will not give us more than we can handle. "No temptation has seized you except what is common to man. And God is faithful; he will not let you be tempted beyond what you can bear. But when you are tempted, he will also provide a way out so that you can stand up under it" (1 Corinthians 10:13). We can turn our fear over to God and he will grant us his peace.

God tells us to fear him: "Now all has been heard; here is the conclusion of the matter: Fear God and keep His commandments, for this is the whole duty of man" (Ecclesiastes 12:13). This is because he has given us rules for our own good. He wants to protect us from harm. But beyond fearing him, God tells us not to dwell on fear, but rather to rely upon him for our security: "But now this is what the Lord says—he who created you, O Jacob, he who formed you, O Israel: 'Fear not, for I have redeemed you; I have called you by name, you are mine'" (Isaiah 43:1).

Fear should not be an obstacle in the development of intimacy in our relationships. We can conquer our fear of expressing anger, or having others express anger to us, if we put our hand in the hand of the One who has told us not to fear.

Don't Cower—Confront!

God gives us the gift of anger, and he will help us overcome feelings of fear as we learn to express our anger. But we need to trust our God-given feelings as helpful. If we do not deny our feelings of fear or panic when they buffet us, they will not overwhelm us.

Instead of cowering because we fear expressing anger, we must confront that fear and conquer it. We need to feel the fear, talk about it, accept it and then go ahead and do what we need to do in spite of it. The following paragraphs provide some guidelines to help you move past your fear to productive anger expression.

Build on a Secure Foundation

Before we can begin to fight for intimacy, we need to be assured that the foundation of love is firmly under our feet. Since anger expression is often a threat to one's sense of personal worth, we must review the reality of our lovableness and self-worth. Ask yourself the following questions: Did I receive enough love as a child? Did my mother love me? Did my father love me? If you can answer yes to these questions, you have a secure foundation for exploring your feelings.

If your parents were not the foundational source of love in your life, who did love you? Your grandparents? Your uncle or aunt? Often, people other than our parents have contributed strongly to our sense of well-being and our feeling of being lovable.

My grandfather adored me; I was the apple of his eye. He thought I was special, and I knew it. Whenever I feel upset and threatened, I retreat to the memories of my grandfather's love for me, and I am restored. Each of us has memories of special people to fall back upon for strength to love ourselves and to take emotional risks. If you can focus on those who loved you and trust that their love was based on your worth, you have a solid platform on which to build. When you are afraid, the love of others will comfort you.

Sometimes, however, the fear of taking emotional risks cannot be easily overcome. Some of us are too defensive to let down our guard and experience our deep anger. If we did not receive enough love as children, our basic security level is insufficient to risk being angry and having others be angry with us in return.

Therefore some of us will live without knowing the satisfaction of intimate contact with others through expressing our deep feelings. This is not the end of the world. Many of our ancestors lived without expressing their feelings, and they enjoyed their lives. However, we are fortunate today that we have the opportunity to choose to be open, and we are learning better ways of communicating. We do need to remember that openness is not a life-threatening decision; it is a life-enhancing choice.

The only major difficulty created by openness between partners is when one member in a relationship chooses openness and the other chooses not to be open because of fear. Often if one partner is growing in a willingness to share, his or her willingness rubs off on the partner at home, and they gradually work out their differences. Occasionally, however, the conflict between expression versus non-expression may lead to a heart-breaking divorce.

Individuals within a relationship are usually on the same emotional level. That's how they found each other in the first place. Often two partners with different levels of expressiveness can find common ground in their emotional unity for building toward mutual openness. If the more open partner is patient, and the less open partner is willing to grow, new levels of openness can be achieved for both of them.

Bob and Ann: Finding Emotional Common Ground. In the beginning Ann loved the self-examination of therapy and took to the idea of being more open like a duck takes to water. But Bob did not like talking about his feelings. Instead he scoffed at Ann's early attempts to share her feelings with him. On the surface Bob and Ann appeared to be mismatched as husband and wife.

However, after a year Bob began to open up, and Ann became the fearful one. When Bob learned to release his anger, Ann wasn't ready for it and needed to adjust. But gradually they moved more deeply into expressing their feelings. Sometimes Bob led the way, and sometimes Ann led.

One day Ann purposely opened up to Bob as he watered the yard: "Bob, I'd like you to spend more time with me. It seems like you're always busy helping other people or keeping busy with chores."

"Now Ann," Bob responded, "did your therapy group coach you to say that? You should know by now that you're important to me. I shouldn't have to tell you."

"Sometimes I don't feel it, Bob. I think you take me for granted. I feel lonely sometimes, and I wish you'd tell me about your feelings for me in your own words."

"If you want me to be truthful about my feelings, you may not always want to hear what I have to say," Bob answered angrily. "You say you want time with me, but you're often out with your friends. I don't see you taking an interest in what I'm doing."

After attempting to fend Ann off, Bob finally told her how he really felt. Ann took a risk and Bob responded on a similar emotional level. No doubt she felt some fear as she met Bob as an equal.

They experienced a difficult period of time while they

adjusted to this new way of relating. They had some bumpy arguments. But each time they fought they felt a little better. They began to appreciate how good they felt with each other afterward. Ann's heart stopped pounding so hard, and Bob didn't get clammy palms any more. The excitement of the closeness they gained from the confrontations offset some of their fear.

Give Yourself Permission to Fight

Another way to overcome the fear of expressing anger is to consciously tell yourself that it is okay to verbalize your anger. You may have been told all your life that you were bad when you were angry. That message is wrong, but it has probably dug a deep groove in your mind which is not easily filled in. You must dig a new groove by continually affirming to yourself that your anger and its constructive expression is good.

By giving ourselves permission to fight and deciding to follow good fighting rules, we can conquer fear and build confidence to express anger. Patient practice of positive confrontation skills also improves our ability to overcome our fear.

At first, all that seems necessary for positive anger expression is a bit of support from others and permission from yourself. Later, as you go deeper into anger expression, the pace will be slower, and you will have setbacks along the way.

When I first gave myself permission to be angry I felt excited and strong. But I do remember overdoing it with my mother. Since I believed it was good to tell the truth, I decided to tell her the whole truth all the time. Later I learned to tell her one thing at a time, and then we could both handle the change. When you move at the proper pace, you won't be overcome with fright!

Use Your Head First

Another guideline for eliminating fear of anger is to

begin with an intellectual approach. In my practice my colleagues and I start by explaining the reasons why people need to express anger. We identify resentments from past and present relationships to help raise the clients' awareness about what bothers them. We also reassure them that it is normal and natural to be angry, and it is good to communicate those feelings openly. Then we slowly lead up to the actual expression of anger.

Most people find focusing on feelings scary. Even talking about our feelings is threatening. Sometimes a therapy program which stresses an intellectual rather than an emotional approach is a good place for the fearful to begin. Many people come to our emotional expression sessions after being in two or three other counseling settings which allayed their fears with the facts about anger expression. Their intellectual pursuits have readied them for exploring their deeper feelings.

June: Building Courage. June came to me at a time of personal crisis. She had been married to Troy for 18 years, and during their entire married life she had been afraid to disagree directly with him. Troy ruled the roost and was bullish in his manner.

June had been raised to believe that a wife should please her husband and never cross him. Nevertheless, finally she reached the breaking point when she could no longer tolerate his disrespect for her. Yet even then it was difficult for her to disagree with him. She felt frozen with fear. Her mother had trained June to avoid anger in relationships with men, teaching her to cater to them instead.

I told June she had a right to be upset and angry as well as a right to express how she felt. We started by giving her permission to *not* smile. She was used to smiling when she felt angry. (She nervously laughed during her first attempt to say "I am angry!") We reviewed the various upsetting situations in her life. Finally, one day the following conversation took place.

Troy came to June to complain about how she handled their rebellious teenager, Eileen. After a lecture from Troy, June mustered her courage and spoke.

"Troy, I don't like the rude way you talk to me. You get an edge in your voice like I'm a stupid child. I agree I shouldn't let Eileen take the car. I wish you would handle some of these situations. You send her to me, but then criticize what I say."

"What's the matter with you tonight?" Troy answered sarcastically.

June continued. "Right now you are being sarcastic. You either talk down to me, or else you don't talk to me at all. I want you to respect me."

After a long pause Troy answered, "I don't know what to say. I'm surprised at you. You seem different. I will think about what you said."

For the first time June did not "take the bait" from her husband, who usually led her to believe something was wrong with her. She was able to continue making her point. It was a strong beginning for many interactions yet to come.

Unfortunately, Troy and June did divorce finally. But the step June took that day to interact more strongly with Troy gave her the courage to stand on her own two feet when she realized she was not going to achieve what she wanted in her relationship with him. Pushing through her fear to say what she thought gave her positive feelings about herself.

Bring Anger to the Surface

Too often we fearfully hide from our anger and ignore the rumblings of our angry feelings. Many times we wait until the rumble becomes a roar before we speak up. Sadly, pent up feelings of anger are often released in a destructive explosion instead of a constructive confrontation.

We need to practice feeling angry and expressing anger to dispel our fear and be comfortable with our anger. We need to take the time to notice our anger, to consciously bring it to the surface and to release it. We will not have a strong feeling about ourselves or our relationships unless we voice our resentments.

It is good for us to take a few minutes each day to ask, "How do I feel?" If you realize that you are annoyed, then that is the time to release the pressure the annoyance causes.

In Emotional Expression Therapy we have a simple but effective way for clients to release their anger. It's called "hitting the stump." We have in our office several old, dead tree stumps. We teach our clients to overcome fear and gradually experience anger by hitting the stumps with rolled-up magazines. Early in the therapy program, I invite the people I counsel to express some of their resentments toward the important people in their lives by hitting the stump and verbalizing their anger at the same time. We state clearly that this is not an act of violence, but rather an exploration of our own anger. We are not hitting another person; we are feeling and releasing our own anger.

The stump gauges how willing an individual is to explore deep feelings. The stump symbolizes the clients' anger. If people are immediately willing to hit the stump, their fear of expressing anger is not disabling, and the anger diminishes perceptibly. Even a few light taps on the stump and a whispered statement show an openness to work on anger expression, even though some fear may be present.

Sometimes a client flatly refuses to have anything to do with the stump stating, "You'll never get me to do that." We have discovered that the resistant person's fear of anger is overwhelming. He or she may not be willing to work on deeper feelings and may leave therapy because of fear.

The stump is a safe way to help someone begin to explore buried anger. We go slowly at first, working from just a few seconds of casual annoyance to several minutes of deep anger over a period of weeks or months.

You can develop your own "hit the stump" method at home for releasing anger. Perhaps you will use a tennis racket on the bed or a rolled-up magazine or newspaper on an old table. At first you may feel self-conscious or afraid because your parents wanted you to keep anger out of sight. But if you will press on through your fear, you will experience the flow of your angry feelings. Once you become accustomed to hitting the stump, you will find yourself feeling strong and relieved.

As you hit the stump, talk to the person as though he or she is there. Make your comments personal and specific. For example, Mary was angry with her mother. As she hit the stump she said, "Mom, I'm angry that you threatened to walk away from me when I was just a little kid. I'm angry that you wouldn't speak to me when I did something wrong. You wouldn't tell me what I did wrong, so I had to guess. I wasn't a bad kid, Mom, but you treated me like I was a bad kid. I need you to love me and to tell me I'm good. I love you and need you."

By hitting the stump, Mary was not rejecting her mother. Anger and its expression is only one part of a good relationship. After expressing her anger, Mary experienced hurt for her mother and then more warmth than ever before.

After we bring our anger to the surface, we feel animated and alive. Anger expression adds zest to our lives. Our fear goes away after we strongly feel our anger and say we are angry. It is impossible to experience fear and anger at the same time. Once you begin to express anger, the fear goes away.

Chapter Five

Get in Touch With Past Family Patterns of Anger

"Honor your father and your mother, so that you may be live long in the land the Lord your God is giving you."

Exodus 20:12

We are the products of our families, and we reflect what we learned at home. Exposure to poor modeling for handling anger during our growing-up years is a major stumbling block to our personal development for expressing anger. Each of us reenacts our parents' expression (or lack of expression) of feelings. We must explore past family patterns for expressing anger to understand our personal difficulties with anger expression and to select better ways of communicating our feelings of displeasure.

We all feel anger toward our parents for the bad things they did in raising us. All parents are far from perfect. To truly honor our parents as God wants us to, we must get to the bottom of our grievances with them. Then we are free to feel our hurt with them followed by a deeper love than ever before. As we heal up our "sore spots" we are open to appreciating them all the more. So our goal in expressing resentments with our parents is to become closer to them.

We also want to be able to choose new, better ways of expressing our anger.

Every generation must go through this process. Our children are coming to my husband and me now. They are angry at some of the bad fights we had before we learned constructive arguing. They are angry for some of our methods of punishing them. This experience is both painful and healing. God works all these things to the good eventually.

Our parents trained us, either directly or indirectly, to remain loyal to them and to their ways of doing things. It's hard work to go against the grain. As adults, many of us find it difficult to form new patterns of behavior even though we realize our parents' methods were inappropriate or unproductive. Thus we tend to perpetuate their methods of dealing with angry feelings, even if their methods were wrong.

After learning the skills of anger expression, we still need time to build confidence in ourselves and to learn how to express our feelings in ways different from our parents. This is especially true when we plan to express anger to our parents in ways which are foreign to them. Our new, positive patterns for anger expression will face their greatest test against the time-honored patterns we grew up with.

Several areas related to family patterns for anger expression must be personally evaluated if we are to develop into open, expressive adults. This chapter will explain a number of the most significant areas.

Talk About the Important Issues

Most of us grew up in families that were afraid to discuss upsetting topics, including feelings of anger. Avoidance is one of the most prominent family patterns which prevents us from expressing anger properly. We need to be able to let our hair down with our family members and discuss our feelings openly and honestly. The family unit is intended to be our refuge from the world—a place we can go to feel loved and accepted no matter what is happening to us.

As adults we are tempted to put our best foot forward when we see our family for a get-together. It's so easy to gather for dinner, chit-chat on pleasant topics and then go home without saying anything important. Talking about feelings of anger often seems counterproductive to family unity.

No one said going against comfortable family norms is easy. Our families may strongly resist discussing the knotty topics we introduce. We must be patient if we are going to bring up and talk through feelings about a family secret such as Dad's alcoholism. It may take many conversations over a period of time to reach a meaningful level on a family topic. Take small steps and keep working on it steadily. Patience and endurance triumph in the end.

Marsha: Talking on a Deeper Level. Marsha's family adopted a flippant attitude toward touchy topics in order to keep interactions superficial. Unpleasant subjects, like Marsha's feelings about her parents' divorce, were smothered by other family members. Her family's pattern of repression was so strong that Marsha felt wrong for rocking the boat. She felt like a bad girl. In therapy Marsha was encouraged to bring these issues to the surface. But it took Marsha many deliberate steps and repeated encouragement in therapy to reach a deeper level of conversation with her family.

For example, one day Marsha was washing the dishes as her mother fixed dessert. Marsha said, "I felt hurt and angry as a teenager when you decided to leave Dad. You never even asked me what *I* wanted."

"Well, that was a long time ago, and it all worked out fine," her mother answered cheerfully. "We've all had hard times, but I think our separating was for the best."

"Mom, I feel put down that you brush over my feelings. I'm disappointed that you are unwilling to hear how I feel."

"Don't dwell on bad feelings, Marsha. Let's talk about your wedding plans."

If her mother had listened and said, "I understand," Marsha would have felt satisfied.

At other times Marsha's father and brother would tease her to prevent her from expressing her feelings. Often this would happen without words. For example, Marsha would say, "I'm upset that you don't take me seriously," and her brother would tickle her until the subject was dropped.

Another example occurred at her wedding rehearsal as Marsha and her father were practicing walking down the aisle together. She was feeling tearfully sad and joyful at the same time. Her father, hoping to avert an emotional exchange, started hobbling like he was an old man. Everyone laughed at his clowning and the vulnerable moment passed.

Finally, after six different attempts at talking about her parents' breakup, Marsha was able to get her family to respond. Her family became increasingly willing to talk about their feelings. As the years pass they continue to go deeper in their willingness to be open and share past hurts.

Roles Can Hinder Communication

In childhood we learned to play the traditional male/female roles. Girls grew up playing with dolls and tending a make-believe home while boys played with cars and fought battles. We traditional women were trained to please our men superficially while actually emotionally running the show at home with our children. We are allowed to cry and be warm but not to get angry. Traditional men were coached to be strong, silent providers and protectors—rocks in troubled times. Only occasionally are men permitted to release their emotions by bellowing, admitting they feel uncertain, or shedding a tear.

Actually, the emotional needs of women and men are very similar. Over my years of counseling I see how alike men and women are. We all get angry, hurt and need love.

Both sexes need to express the whole range of feelings often. All of us, regardless of gender, possess emotional strengths and insecurities. Husbands and wives need to share openly their everyday problems and successes to be close companions. In recent years women have entered the work place in large numbers, and much has been discussed and written about the equality of women and their changing roles. Some changes have indeed come about. Men are spending more time with their children, doing housework and cooking. Women have learned more about coping with the world and handling finances.

In mentioning these changes I am not simply describing outward behaviors but rather how they reflect changed inner emotional beliefs. In our hearts we still see men as responsible for providing and women as taking care of the family. Old attitudes die hard.

The man is the head of the household, as the Bible says. Yet within that framework there should be the utmost mutual respect between husband and wife. Neither is more important than the other. The amount of money each partner earns should have no bearing on the power they wield. Ideally each has equal influence; for example, the wife should have input on money decisions and the husband on care of their child. Each needs to be capable of nurturing the children or managing the business of the family. Such understanding gives both the man and the woman more love. There is freedom in breaking out of confining roles!

To determine whether our emotional responses are honest or programmed by traditional roles, we need to ask ourselves some serious questions. Do we respond emotionally from habit, or do we openly release our deeper feelings? Do we automatically assume that the opposite sex feels differently about an issue, or do we recognize the similarities in our feelings? Do prejudices operate in our thoughts, or do we respond as one person to another? As we develop the freedom to react as individuals rather than as actors in established roles, we will be closer and more appreciative in our opposite-sex relationships.

Ben and Darlene: Dropping Male/Female Roles. Darlene and Ben were trained by their respective families to accept traditional male/female roles: strong, dominant males and soft, feminine females. Both had difficulties in their childhood homes.

Darlene was adopted a few days after birth, but her adoptive parents divorced when she was just a few years old. Her mother was an alcoholic and unable to care for her, so Darlene was passed around the family until her adoptive father remarried. For a few years Darlene lived with her grandmother because her stepmother was jealous of her close relationship with her father.

Both of Ben's parents were killed in an accident when he was four years old. The family lawyer took Ben into his home and adopted him. The family was strict, their expectations of Ben were high, and warmth and affection were minimal. Ben was rebellious, but he learned to fit into the family mold in order to survive. He never felt completely at ease with his adoptive family.

Darlene and Ben met in grammar school and married in their late teens. Having endured insecure childhoods, both Ben and Darlene craved the security of a stable, traditional home. Darlene cooked well, was an excellent seamstress and enjoyed caring for their son, Mike. Ben became a model provider and protector in his job as a paramedic. Ben liked to fish with his buddies, and Darlene spent much time visiting with her female friends.

Darlene and Ben came to see me because they were failing to meet each other's emotional needs. In pursuing their separate traditional role identities they lost their identity as an understanding, caring couple. They had little uninterrupted time together since Ben was on call every other weekend and frequently worked twelve-hour shifts.

Often Ben would try to sleep while Darlene would attempt to keep Mike quiet. When they *were* around each other, Ben would be watching a game on TV or out in the garage working on a project. Darlene would be in the kitchen or at her sewing machine. Even on Sunday morning Ben went alone to the early service, so he could relax the rest of the day around the house. Darlene and Mike went later so Mike could go to Sunday school and because Darlene "loved the music."

They didn't even go to bed or get up together. Ben said he wasn't tired enough to fall sleep when Darlene felt exhausted from getting up at 6 a.m. each day. She would go to bed two hours before him, but he often stayed in bed till 7:30 in the morning. They were like ships passing in the night. No wonder they felt lonely and unloved.

They needed their separate identities, but they also needed to be involved with each other in a loving relationship. They needed to experience their individual strengths when they were with each other, not just when they pulled away and participated in separate activities.

The best way to feel powerful in a relationship is to let your partner know when and how you disagree. If you restrict anger expression to the traditional male/female roles, you rob your partner of the depth of the relationship. For example, if Ben gets angry with Darlene because she spends too much time talking on the phone, he may not feel free to express his anger because a woman's role is to cook, clean and talk on the phone. If Darlene gets angry with Ben for going fishing, she may restrict her criticism because a man's role is to provide, protect and go fishing.

But in reality, being angry with a partner for any reason and failing to express that anger is dishonest. No wonder Darlene and Ben were having trouble; they had allowed their roles to cheat them out of a vital dimension of their relationship.

With some encouragement, this couple began confronting each other. After the first fear passed, they became good fighters, mutually strong and verbal. They both started to enjoy the reward of feeling powerful and satisfied, which made each succeeding fight easier to broach.

Darlene wanted Ben to go bike riding with her. Ben didn't want Darlene to sew at nights and on weekends. Each of them missed the cuddling in bed at night and were surprised they both felt the same way! They agreed to sit together each day for an *uninterrupted* fifteen minutes. During that time they would say what they felt, what they liked and didn't like about their relationship with each other that day.

They also planned to set aside one night each week for a date night and took turns planning it. After many talks they resolved that Darlene would go to the early church service once a month, and Ben would keep Darlene and Mike company the rest of the time. Ben was touched that Darlene *wanted* him to be the spiritual leader of the family.

Once they kicked away the egg shells they had been walking on, they made many changes. Ben spent more time caring for Mike and enjoyed fixing a meal several times a week. Darlene sat down to watch an occasional basketball game and helped Ben with part of the yard work. They felt satisfied with their companionship.

Relieved of their role restrictions, Ben and Darlene are both aware of more options and freedom. Furthermore, they see how similar they are: they experience the same fears, frustrations, anger, hurt and warmth. They feel equally important in expressing themselves.

Poor Childhood Experiences With Anger

When some of us were children, perhaps our parents could not accept our expressions of anger because they were uncomfortable with their own anger, as maybe our grandparents were uncomfortable with their anger. Dislike of anger seems to be perpetuated from generation to generation.

When I was angry as a child my mother said, "Go to your room until you can be a nice girl!" Even worse, sometimes she shouted, "Stop your yelling!" and then gave me a spanking for raising *my* voice.

With mixed messages like these we came to see anger as something ugly which must be avoided. I felt the tension as my parents held back their anger. I was uneasy as I heard the complaining, felt the sarcasm and saw the dirty looks. My mother would clench her teeth and say to my father, "I think you'll ruin those pants in the garden, but go ahead and do what you want." We all knew there would be trouble later if he did not listen to her. My parents would keep things smooth on the surface but jabbed at each other underneath.

When their once-restrained anger finally did explode, I remember sitting under the dining room table crying, thinking they were going to get a divorce. That was never an issue—they loved each other deeply—but their occasional outbursts terrified me.

I hear many worse stories from my clients, though, about when anger exploded in disrespectful words or actions. They were frightened to hear the mean things their parents screamed at each other. They feared that they would start throwing things or hitting each other. Frequently clients report that their parents *did* physical fighting. Often abusive fighting is a part of addiction patterns. I believe all families are dysfunctional to some extent—handed down from generation to generation, from original sin.

Because of such poor experiences with destructive family fighting as children, it is difficult for us to argue as adults. If the anger you witnessed as a child resulted in bitter rejection, physical brawls and unhappy endings, no wonder you don't want anything to do with it now!

Destructive fighting, past and present, can lead to fear of anger. Fear of anger is a healthy fear and couples need to deal with it by committing themselves to the basic rules for constructive fighting. Chapter 6 of this book will introduce you to some rules for fair, positive fighting.

Ron and Harriet: Dropping Intimidation. Ron and Harriet have been married for more than thirty years. For most of that time Harriet was afraid of Ron's explosive temper. Ron himself was afraid of his anger. Neither of them were willing to fight about their differences until they began therapy.

Harriet's childhood family had a pattern of keeping relationships smooth and unruffled. Her family members were nice, superficial people who repaid hurts by withdrawing and staying private.

Ron's father hit him as a child. If Ron did anything wrong he was punished with a "lickin'." Ron's fear of his father was justified because his father would lose control and lash out violently. Like many whipped children, Ron protected his father and would not speak ill of him. Even when encouraged in therapy to be angry about his father's cruel discipline, Ron continued to minimize the harmful punishment he had received. In protecting his father Ron was actually protecting himself from the hurt he felt about his harsh treatment as a boy and the harsh treatment he, in turn, gave to his children.

Ron bragged about being tough when he was a kid. He frequently fought at school and with his brothers. He started many fights to defend a person who was being picked on. He would protect underdogs and feel sad for them, but he would not let himself feel hurt about any of his own injuries. He would not even let himself feel the sadness of losing his front teeth in a fist fight.

Because he didn't allow himself to feel hurt, he didn't take good care of himself. He was afraid that the hurt would obliterate his self-esteem, so he maintained a tough-guy front. As an adult he was oblivious to the danger of being thirty pounds overweight and drinking two six-packs of beer a day.

Ron's children were a tough bunch of kids, used to physical fighting. They talked big and got into trouble. Once his son was suspended from school for cutting classes and talking disrespectfully to his teacher. Ron dealt with Steve the same way his father had handled him—with physical abuse. There were times when Ron was so angry with his son he would pummel him. Harriet would watch silently, afraid to intervene.

Because of the beatings they received, the men in Ron's family found it difficult to feel good about themselves. They had trouble respecting themselves. Yet they put up a tough front, insisting they liked their lives as they were. Denial was their best defense.

In therapy Ron was finally able to reveal how he felt about his treatment of Steve. He felt responsible for many of his son's problems. He also began to admit that his own father had been unnecessarily rough on him. As Ron was able to talk more openly about his childhood beatings, his fear about losing control of his anger began to diminish.

In turn Harriet realized she needed to be more courageous in standing up to Ron and in fighting with him. He had never hit her, and he was now willing to make the commitment that he never would. She felt guilty and hurt that she had not been brave enough to speak out against Ron's harsh treatment of Steve. She also needed to admit her complicity in Ron's behavior—goading Ron with words like a bullfighter provokes a bull with a red cape. As she talked about her fear of anger Harriet revealed that her uncle had molested her when she was six years old. Her feelings of helplessness stemmed from that traumatic experience.

Both of them believed in God though neither had a personal relationship with their Father in prayer. As they hit the bottom of their painful experiences I encouraged them to pray, asking the Lord to heal them, to give them courage to feel and express their feelings, and to help them be willing to forgive those who had deeply hurt them. I watched their faith increase as the Holy Spirit transformed their defensiveness and pain into love and peace.

After they began talking constructively about their disrespectful fighting, both Harriet and Ron felt better about themselves and more capable of learning to express their anger in a healthy manner. They had compassion for each other because of what they had been through. Together they were willing to evaluate their fights and continue to improve their methods.

Constructive arguments helped them feel much closer. Instead of being antagonists, they became a loving team. Eventually they were able to have several family sessions in which they admitted their mistakes to their children, asking their forgiveness. They all cried together. God granted them a fresh start. The children now have the opportunity to be different with their future families.

It's Okay to Fight in Front of the Children

If we fight well, we do better to fight in front of our children than to hide our anger from them. If we fight respectfully, we do not need to be ashamed of our anger. Children are more frightened by the distressing noise from the other room than by being in the same room and hearing the words. If you are part of a family, fight together! If it happens naturally, let everyone know what is going on. Exposure to constructive expressions of anger at an early age will help our children accept anger as a healthy, normal part of living. Initially, they may be frightened by anger and may want to run away or cry. Yet they quickly adapt as soon as it becomes clear that we parents are closer after a constructive fight.

After parents develop a pattern of fighting well in front of their children, the youngsters will often become nonchalant about fights and will go on eating dinner or watching television during the exchange. Good fighting and parental support are the two most important ingredients in helping children accept disagreements as a normal part of life.

Actually, expressing anger is much easier for children than it is for adults since children have not yet learned to shut their feelings down. Children are often the ones to hear and feel a fight coming on before their parents will admit to being angry. My daughter would pick up the early clues and say to my husband and me, "Are you two going to fight again tonight?"

Children are full-fledged persons in their own right, and it is detrimental to treat them as though they are too fragile. They understand much more than we give them credit for, and they are much more upset by our attempts to hide something from them than by what they see and hear.

Many times in family sessions I see children who act as if they are ignoring what their parents are saying to each other; however, these youngsters are actually soaking in every detail of the adult conversation. As soon as there is a shift in feelings, the children's behavior adjusts accordingly.

When parents are angry I have seen children (a) start a commotion to distract them; (b) stand in the corner and suck their fingers; (c) plead with their parents, saying things like "don't fight;" (d) cling to their parents' legs. Even small babies are astute. One crawled over and bit her mother's leg when Mom yelled at her brother. Another eight-month-old dirtied her pants just before Mom and Dad's argument launched into high gear.

As parents we generally overprotect our children. We try not to fight around the children because we do not want them to be upset. This is a reaction to the hurt we experienced as children which we have not learned to accept as a good part of who we are. But when we overprotect our children, they are not exposed to the hurt they need to grow emotionally and to accept all facets of their lives.

We need to interrupt unhealthy family patterns of denial and overprotection and bring anger into the open as an accepted part of our family lives. The key is admitting that constructive fighting is good for the whole family to experience. With this excellent modeling, our children will not need years of therapy to help them overcome their inhibitions and distortions.

Rick and Kate: "Perfect" Parents. Rick and Kate tried hard to be perfect parents. They worked at giving their children, Mike and Sandy, every opportunity to grow and be secure. They provided their children with a comfortable home, were involved in their schools and church, and offered them a variety of constructive activities. Their baby sitters were carefully selected to enrich their children's lives, and the door was open for their friends to come and go. The one area in which Mike and Sandy did not enjoy an advantage, however, was in the development of their emotional expression.

When Rick and Kate first started counseling, they did not tell their children they were going to therapy. They never argued or displayed upset feelings in front of Mike and Sandy. When Rick and Kate were not getting along they masked their feelings and acted as though nothing were wrong. Kate would cuddle and baby the children to smooth over her uncomfortable feelings. Rick was cheerful and efficient with Mike and Sandy so they would not know he was in pain. In particular, Rick wanted to shield Mike from his difficulties with Kate since he did not believe Mike was as strong as Sandy.

But Sandy sensed something was wrong between her parents and began to cause trouble to get attention. She was unconsciously pushing them to work on their relationship. She would show off, noisily calling attention to herself to get Mom and Dad involved. Mike, on the other hand, used silence and withdrawal to attract attention. He would act shy and be unwilling to talk about himself, which caused Rick and Kate to worry about him.

I recommended that Rick and Kate not only be natural

and do their fighting around the children as anger came up, but also that they take an active role in teaching and demonstrating good fighting skills to their children. I emphasized that as parents they were not encouraging Mike and Sandy's emotional growth by hiding the truth from them.

It was difficult for Rick and Kate to drop their cloak of privacy. However, they gradually did by practicing at home. Mike and Sandy were very interested. During the first argument with all four of them present, Rick and Kate told the children, "Don't worry, we're going to argue but this is good and will help us to feel better with each other." They even discussed the fight rules they were going to practice and suggested that Mike and Sandy tell them afterward if they thought they had abided by the rules.

Sandy had much to say and was eager to talk about her feelings. She embraced emotional expression at the age of eight without batting an eyelash. She loved having a separate therapy session with her mother and felt important and respected as an individual.

Mike had more difficulty expressing himself. He had clearly picked up the message that his father felt weaker in emotional situations and that he expected Mike to feel that way also. At least Mike was getting an early start at talking about feelings, and together Rick and Mike helped each other progress in building emotional confidence.

Sharing their feelings openly brought the four family members closer together. The children gained additional security from knowing what was going on emotionally between all four of them and from being able to discuss their problems. Involvement with each other is healthy for any family; emotional contact between family members is what we all need for satisfaction.

Keep the Children out of the Middle

Sometimes, instead of overprotecting our children as a way of avoiding anger, we drag our children into the middle of our fights and focus our resentments on them. This helps us avoid the greater fear of confronting each other. But it is too heavy a burden for our children to be asked to take sides in our arguments—to become part of the problem instead of seeing us face and resolve the problem. It is good to let children know what is going on without revealing all the gory details. But it is not good to make them responsible for our problems.

Paul and Mary: Hiding Behind Their Daughter. When I first met with Paul and Mary they were a subdued couple. They slumped in their chairs looking pale and drawn.

Paul started out with a long list of complaints about Mary, related as a story without emotion. He saw Mary teaming up with their daughter, Barbara, to ignore Paul. Mary and Barbara would sit together and talk easily, but the conversation stopped when Paul entered the room. Mary was lenient with Barbara and forced Paul into the role of disciplinarian. Paul felt righteously indignant and sorry for himself.

Mary talked in a high-pitched voice, weakly exclaiming that Paul was difficult to please and that she could not help having high blood pressure, which made her unable to work. She emphasized it was not her fault that Barbara had a better relationship with her than with him. She saw Paul as too harsh and unreasonable.

In the early stages of their therapy we could not avoid talking about Barbara. Whatever the topic we could not have a session that did not degenerate into a fight over Barbara. Paul was furious that Mary protected and sided with Barbara. Mary was upset that Paul expected too much and was too critical. I suggested they work on their ability to fight with each other in a constructive, straightforward manner instead of using Barbara as a distraction.

Aside from their arguments with each other about Barbara, Paul and Mary both agreed that their daughter was not doing what they wanted. Mary admitted that as a parent she did not feel as though she had control over Barbara. Barbara did not respect her. If Mary asked Barbara to do a chore, Barbara ignored her. So Mary settled for being Barbara's buddy instead of defending her position as mother. Paul felt defeated by Barbara before he even approached her. Paul wanted Barbara to bring her friends home, which Barbara scornfully refused to do. Both Mary and Paul had given up their parental power to Barbara, and they resented her for not complying with their rules. They needed to become a team, consulting with each other before making any decisions with Barbara.

Paul and Mary were not feeling loved and appreciated by each other, so they tried to get what they were missing from Barbara. Barbara felt overburdened and afraid of all the power they gave her, and she acted up in return. Therefore, the best way for them to improve the situation with their daughter was to get their husband-wife relationship working better. The greatest security we can offer our children is that Dad and Mom are emotionally together. Paul and Mary agreed to become a team, and we went to work.

They both came from insecure backgrounds, and it was clear that they both felt like losers. Their self-esteem was so low that each depended upon the other to feel better. Paul wanted Mary to tell him over and over again how wonderful she thought he was. And Mary wanted Paul to cuddle her, love her and protect her from the world. It seemed that neither of them could meet the other's needs because they were hurting from their own unfulfilled needs. Disappointed in each other and helpless to reach out, they picked on each other in a belittling way and ended up feeling alienated and alone.

Since both of them felt insecure, Paul and Mary were afraid to fight with each other directly. Paul bullied and criticized Mary and Barbara. Mary, keeping her anger underground, felt rebellious toward Paul. She and Barbara, acting like they were both teenagers, banded together against Paul. They had an unspoken agreement not to take responsibility and to drive Paul crazy by not paying attention to his requests. They looked at Paul as the bad guy and blamed him for overreacting.

Once Paul and Mary recognized their disagreements, they agreed that they needed to learn to fight constructively with each other. With slow, steady progress they began to accept anger as a necessary part of their lives.

When Paul and Mary became more actively involved with each other, Barbara was left in peace and quiet for the first time. Her parents were no longer using her as a buffer for their feelings for each other. This was a difficult adjustment for Barbara. She had lost the negative attention she was relying upon.

Fortunately her old tactics gradually faded into more positive actions. She found a part-time job and started studying more seriously. Gradually Barbara learned that the warmth and acceptance she now felt from both her parents more than compensated for the negative attention she had lost. With the pressure off her, she was more cooperative and branched out more independently in her life. In fact, Paul, Mary and Barbara were all able to live their lives without leaning too much on each other. When Barbara was asked how she felt about her mom and dad's therapy work, she was glowing in her response.

"Mom and Dad have a good time with each other now," she said. "I feel good when I see them talking together and holding hands. I don't feel like I have to worry about them anymore. Sometimes I think they're too strict with me but we can talk it over. At least we all agree eventually."

We need to appreciate our families, yet be willing to look at past patterns for handling anger and improve them as necessary. We need to talk on a deeper level about our feelings and knock down the walls that some of the traditional roles have created.

We need to feel our strength as independent persons in our marriages and to treat each other as equals. As family members we need to function as equals in communicating, although mother and father are the final authorities when children are involved. It's best that children learn how to fight constructively. Therefore, good fighting can happen openly as long as the children are not put in the middle. The family that fights together constructively stays together!

Chapter Six

Learn the Rules for Clean Fighting

*"In your anger do not sin": Do not let the sun go
down while you are still angry, and do not give the
devil a foothold ."*

Ephesians 4:26, 27

We need to tell each other the truth, but we also need to
follow constructive guidelines for expressing anger to
prevent our anger from becoming the work of the devil. We
need to use our God-given virtues to express anger without
going over the line and being mauled by the devil. Our
exaggerated anger must be put aside so that we do not reject
the people dear to us.

God's love for us is reflected in our love for each other.
God wants us to live and love in close, committed relationships. He wants our families to be strong and united. For us
to develop closeness and fulfill God's desires, we need to
speak out when we are upset and work out troublesome
issues with those we love.

How we speak out and our approach to an argument must
always reflect our commitment to God and his Word. Prayer
can keep us honest with ourselves and help us view what we
do through God's eyes. Are we being selfish? Are we putting
the other person down? Are we insisting on having our own

way? Are we assuming the attitude that we are better than the other person? Or do we really want to work out a problem? Do we like and love the other person? Do we respect his or her needs? Do we believe he or she is as important as we are? Only when we acknowledge and respect the other person, and subject our arguing to God's light, can our arguing draw us closer to one another and strengthen our love and commitment.

One direct way to express anger is through a constructive fight. A fight is simply an exchange of negative information. The experience of fighting can be as simple as the definition if we do not overreact to anger-producing situations. In a fight two partners are displeased and each is saying why. We are giving each other honest, valuable information about how we feel so that the other person does not have to guess what is wrong with us. The word *exchange* is crucial to our definition because it specifies equal participation. It clarifies from the beginning that both partners are willing to engage in the interaction.

One way we know we've had a constructive argument is that we feel relieved. We feel satisfied we've had our say and feel good about how we said it. We probably feel hurt, but there are no regrets regarding the fight itself.

Each couple needs to establish its own fight regulations in order to feel safe enough to express anger. Anger is scary. Therefore, it is necessary to define clear and specific guidelines that will keep our fighting fair and safe. Some regulations are mandatory, while others may vary from couple to couple. In this chapter we will explore six mandatory rules: (1) show respect for self and others; (2) maintain equality: no winners or losers; (3) fight safely: no violence; (4) be reasonable: no hysterics; (5) be clean and sober: no drugs (including alcohol); and (6) be brief: limit all fights to five minutes.

Regulation 1: Show Respect:
For Self and Others

This first fight regulation paves the way for fair, constructive fighting. We respect each other when we make it clear that we want to work through our differences to end up feeling closer. Each fight must begin with the commitment to value one another above the issues of the exchange.

Our actions, our words and our tone of voice reveal whether we value the other person. Sarcasm, rudeness, putdowns and accusations cause us to react and prevent constructive fighting. If we have a point to make, we need to put it across without diminishing the other person. If we speak plainly and state what is bothering us, we will have an effect on the other person. And if we are respectful, the other person will respect us. We need to treat others as we want to be treated.

Harry and Prudence: Hurling Accusations. When Harry and Prudence first came to see me they were both hurt. They had endured 25 years of marriage in which they felt disrespectful of each other. Their arguments deteriorated quickly into hurling accusations. Harry told Prudence that she was an unexciting sexual partner. She told him he was a rotten father. He said she never listened to him or made him feel attractive. She said he never did what she asked him to do. They made such negative statements about each other that it was hard to have any hope for rebuilding their relationship.

Early in their therapy, one dialogue went like this:

Prudence gave Harry an irritated look and whined, "You were at work all the time, and you left me to take care of the kids as well as everything else at home."

Harry's eyes hardened as he leaned forward, raised his voice angrily and retorted, "You always put the kids ahead of me. I never felt special. Why would I even want to come home? The kids were always crying and you were always complaining."

Prudence continued without acknowledging Harry, "You wouldn't help me with the simplest jobs . . . "

"I don't want to listen to you. You always think you're right," Harry brusquely interrupted.

Changing their lifetime habits of accusing each other required slow, patient work. With encouragement, during therapy they began to talk about each other's good qualities. Both of them healed a little each time a respectful discussion took place. Over time they became more vulnerable. I pointed out that they had married each other for good reasons, and eventually they came to agree.

Several years later the following calm argument took place:"I wish we could talk more," Prudence said casually as she lounged comfortably in her chair. "Sometimes I think we are both missing each other, but we are afraid to admit it."

Harry smiled and added, "You are the person I want to spend my time with, and sometimes I give up when you don't seem interested."

She returned his smile. "But I am interested in you. I still feel excited when I hear your car pull in the driveway!"

"I'm glad you're telling me this. I need to know that you feel that way. There are times I don't feel I can satisfy you," Harry admitted.

Prudence went over to him and pulled him up out of the chair. "I have given you a hard time. I do love you." She hugged him, and he responded warmly.

"I love you, too," he whispered.

The same people, a different approach, and now they are able to *feel* loved. We want to change when we know we're loved.

Regulation 2: Maintain Equality: No Winners or Losers

A constructive fight cannot have winners and losers. The partner who loses feels resentful, defensive and vengeful.

The partner who wins feels proud and superior. There is no way partners can get close if each insists on lording it over the other by trying to win the fight. If a fight has a winner or loser, then a judgment has been made. Many couples enter therapy trapped by competitive feelings about who is right and who is wrong.

Colin and April: Competition. Colin and April were upset when they arrived for their first session. It was obvious April felt Colin was wrong. She had good reasons for being angry with him. He was not working steadily. He was irresponsible around the house. He made sarcastic comments about April around other people. He often flew off the handle with his anger, and sometimes he drank too much.

Before long I could see Colin's part in this couple's win/lose syndrome. When he had the opportunity, Colin wanted the upper hand with April. He "pushed her buttons" by telling her frequently that she was controlling and cold. He reminded her often that she was just like her mother, and he wasn't going to allow her to boss him around like her mother bossed her dad.

Their competition and desire to win fed their anger. If April was not putting Colin down, Colin was putting April down. Unable to see past being right, they each were unable to experience the hurt that would allow them to feel vulnerable and ultimately closer to the other.

Each had met his/her match; there was no way either could get on top and stay there. I gently encouraged them to talk about their hurt without worrying about winning the argument. At first even their hurt was expressed in an accusing manner. But after a few weeks, feeling worn down, hurt and tired of being tough, their voices gradually softened and tears flowed.

Through expressing their hurt, April and Colin became able to hug each other warmly at the end of a fight. The competition slowly waned as the companionship and understanding that resulted from sharing their hurt increased.

Once they saw their relationship as a refuge from the world they began to comfort each other and cheer each other on. They saw that they could both do well at the same time —in fact, they could do better—if they helped each other. They realized they were both on the winning team!

Regulation 3: Fight Safely: No Violence

The third mandatory fight regulation states that there will be no violence or physical intimidation. Violence is a violation of our physical being. By engaging in or tolerating violent behavior we lose respect for ourselves and one another. Both persons end up feeling powerless, frustrated and frightened. Any good point we might make becomes lost behind the shock of a glass being thrown, a shove or a slap. Violence is disrespectful and degrading.

People who think they aren't good with words or who doubt their influence often resort to violence. However, our message is never effective if we resort to violence. Practice using words! A commitment to nonviolence must be made and kept.

Howard and Tina: Explosions. When Howard and Tina first came to see me, little fighting was going on between them, but resentments were building. Tina had given up fighting with Howard because he would intimidate her physically—sometimes slapping her or throwing something near her. Howard felt his violent behavior was justified because Tina could handle words better than he. When he thought she was backing him into a corner with clever arguments, he felt helpless and would erupt into a rage.

Tina had a knack for provoking Howard. But before we could begin to work on Tina's bad habits, we needed to get a commitment from Howard that he would not become violent when fighting. This was not easy since some of their early conversations were painful, as we can see from the following example:

Tina sat slumped in her chair, slightly turned away from Howard. Her eyes were swollen from crying, and she would not look at him. Howard leaned forward. "Talk to me, Tina. Last night was upsetting, but I don't deserve this silent treatment."

She gave him a hard look. "I wish I could do more to hurt you. I hate you for pushing me against the wall last night."

He flinched and countered, "I didn't hurt you. I just kept you from leaving the room."

"You did hurt me, and I feel helpless about it," she said with her voice rising. "You don't even care how I feel. You just want your own way."

Howard raised his voice louder than hers. "You think you are so perfect. I'm tired of you looking down your nose at me. You have an answer for everything. I feel frustrated."

"Before we go further we need to pray," I intervened. We held hands and bowed our heads, "Lord, help us to love each other and to have peace. When we don't love ourselves enough please pour your love on us. Keep us from making the mistake of physically lashing out with our anger. In Jesus' name we pray, amen."

Both Tina and Howard felt helpless. They needed God's help. Howard's commitment to nonviolence would be a big step forward, but he needed to see the value of the commitment for him instead of just giving Tina her way. He needed to see that his violent explosions diverted the issues; he lost the point when he became the problem.

Tina needed to acknowledge that she, too, was being violent by participating in the explosive fights. She could see Howard becoming furious, yet she would press him further. I suggested that they both sign a written commitment to nonviolence.

As we discussed the importance of respect in relationships, Tina and Howard began to identify and appreciate their need for self-respect. They came to realize the necessity of treating each other as they wished to be treated. They began to see violence as an insult leading to a loss of dignity and respect.

After Tina and Howard realized that I was not judging them, they became less defensive and admitted that they needed to drop their self-destructive and defeating roles. Yet both were afraid they would be unable to control their behavior. I assured them that they could, reminding them that there are always a few seconds in which to decide what they are going to do before they do it. They had the power to make a decision and stick with it. It was a matter of taking responsibility for their lives.

They signed the commitment. Each of them prayed a prayer of repentance and asked God for forgiveness. They turned to each other, apologized and asked for forgiveness.

Tina's eyes sparkled as she entered my office with Howard a year later. They were still talking casually with each other as they sat down. She leaned over and placed her hand on Howard's knee saying, "It feels good to be so comfortable with you. I feel I can bring up anything I want to. I can remember when I had to be careful how I worded things."

"I feel better, too," Howard said. "I feel good when you're talking to me. And I'm glad we can both get angry and express it positively."

Tina and Howard learned to stick with their commitment. Over a period of a year, trust grew between them. Feeling good about himself, Howard was able to let in the extra warmth and openness from Tina that resulted from their commitment. Once their catastrophic fears had been eliminated, they were able to feel proud of their fights.

Not all of their fights were easy. They had to take many small steps in a constant struggle toward clean fighting. Sometimes they fell back into old patterns and would have to get back on track. Most importantly, though, deep in their hearts they had decided that they wanted a good relationship.

Regulation 4: Be Reasonable: No Hysterics

Hysteria is another way of overdoing our feelings. Such overindulgence makes it impossible to have a clean fight. Hysterics are the result of feeling overwhelmed. If we do not feel powerful, we sometimes panic and give up effective control of our emotions.

Becoming hysterical always makes us feel worse instead of better. Our self-esteem does a nose-dive. We know we have made a mistake and need to apologize. Our point has been lost in the shuffle because hysteria has become the main issue. We feel weak with shame. But we do have the split second to decide whether to be hysterical or not. We can control this behavior.

Dan and Barbara: Going Overboard. Dan and Barbara were afraid to fight with each other. Barbara didn't trust her feelings, and she would panic in an argument with Dan. She would stop listening and make off-the-wall comments that gave Dan the feeling that she might go crazy.

Dan learned to walk on tiptoe around her, but resentment built up inside of him from holding back. To make matters worse, Barbara would goad Dan into a fight because she felt uneasy about the tension. When a fight would erupt Dan would overdo his anger, bellowing much louder and longer than necessary. Barbara would sob and scream and make extreme statements. They experienced some bad exchanges, such as the following episode:

Dan and Barbara glared at each other across the dinner table. Dan suddenly stood up, threw his napkin across the table and said loudly, "I've had it. You are a cold fish. Trying to be close to you is like hugging an iceberg."

Barbara blanched and began to tremble. Her eyes flashed anger as she lashed out, "You're right, I don't care about you.

I've never even been attracted to you. I just want you to leave me alone!"

"You bet I'll leave you alone," he continued. "I can find myself a real woman; someone who doesn't have all your hang-ups."

"All you want is sex!" she screamed. "You're so grouchy and moody, and then all of a sudden you just want my body. You're disgusting." She threw his napkin back at him.

He knocked his chair out of the way. "Just stay away from me," he yelled over his shoulder as he stamped away. "I'm going to pour myself a drink."

Both Dan and Barbara knew that battle lines were drawn and that it would take a week or two before they would treat each other decently again. Meanwhile, each stubbornly suffered.

After an initial fight they would both lapse into icy silence, ignoring each other except for monosyllabic responses. They would sleep on the opposite edges of their bed as the invisible wall between them loomed large.

Each needed to work on removing panic reactions to anger. Barbara was so afraid of anger that she became hysterical. She would either shout back or hyperventilate and want to flee. A few days after a fight she would feel sorry, but she didn't believe she could stop having her initial reaction to anger. Over and over again I assured her that I knew she could. There are always those few seconds in which we can make the decision to either say how we feel or to overreact.

After a while Barbara made a commitment not to become hysterical. It was difficult for her and she needed support. Several times she broke the commitment but quickly remade it. Each time she felt a little more in control and better able to see what she was doing. Hysteria is not black and white; it is gray. She needed to find the point where she could express herself fully without going too far. Finally, she did.

Dan and Barbara continued to seesaw. If Dan was in a

cooperative mood, Barbara was upset and unwilling to work. If Barbara was eager to express herself well, then Dan was being cold and indifferent. It was difficult to find them willing to work with each other at the same time.

As Barbara improved, it became easier to see Dan's more subtle forms of hysteria, and attention was then directed to him. When Dan was upset, he would become moody and withdrawn. If he didn't want to express his feelings, there was no budging him.

Dan and Barbara continued to take turns being impossible with each other even while they were working on their individual issues. As is often the case, their destructive patterns grew worse before getting better. It took six months before they softened toward each other. The hurt they were finally willing to share made a big difference because it gave each of them the level of support they needed.

They also learned to compliment each other as they made progress. Neither of them was used to being told good things about themselves, so they didn't make positive statements about others. This took an attitude change, new vocabulary and lots of practice. Finally they dropped their overreaction to each other, and their "no hysterics" commitment became valid.

Regulation 5: Be Clean and Sober: No Drugs (Including Alcohol)

All drugs distort our feelings to some extent. Therefore, it is important not to fight while taking any drugs. This includes alcohol, marijuana, cocaine or any prescription or nonprescription drug. (Even cigarettes, coffee and aspirin will change our natural feelings.) I will use alcohol as the example here since it is the most common problem drug. What I say about alcohol applies to any other addiction.

Anger plus alcohol can be ugly and often leads to violence. Alcohol blurs our better judgment. Often people mistakenly think that alcohol's ability to lower our inhibitions is positive. I view it as a negative by-product since our inhibitions can protect us from abandoning our basic values.

Alcohol frequently becomes an issue when I help couples improve their communication. If alcohol is a problem for them they are usually defensive. Often both partners will band together to protect their drinking. Some of the defensive comments are:

"We only have a few drinks each night and never after 9 or 10 p.m."

"We never drink until evening."

"We don't drink hard liquor—only beer or wine."

"We *hardly ever* drink too much."

"My drinking doesn't affect me; it just helps me relax."

I believe all of the above statements can indicate a problem. If we are watching our drinks and worrying about the issue of alcohol, we should be relieved to get alcohol out of our lives. The distinction between problem drinking and alcoholism seems superfluous to me. If we have a problem with our drinking and continue to drink, we are out of control with alcohol. If we have a problem in our relationships we shouldn't drink.

It is ironic that people choose to drink when they are around their most intimate partners. All day long they have been clear-headed, but when the time comes to interact in their relationships they drink. Their feelings and thoughts become blurred, and their personalities are altered.

Jean and Tom: Alcohol Upheavals. Jean and Tom met through close friends. Getting involved in a relationship seemed scary to them because of their prior relationships. Jean's previous marriage had been brief, but it left a big scar on her. Tom's marriage had lasted 15 years. They were both willing to try therapy.

The first problems to surface were resentments stemming from Tom's acting bossy and Jean's responding rebelliously. He related to Jean as though he were the wise, all-knowing solver of her problems. But Tom did not share his problems with Jean. He appeared to have everything under control.

Jean resented Tom's checking up on her the way her father had done years before. She often got back at Tom in devious ways. For example, she "forgot" his birthday and came an hour late to his office party. Sometimes she withdrew, drank vodka and rudely cut him off.

When Tom felt resentment toward Jean he did not express it. He continued to pamper Jean, then he withdrew to his house, got drunk and refused to see her. After a few days, weeks or sometimes months, he recovered enough to resume his relationship with Jean. Even then he would not want to talk about what had happened. He was defensive and quick to point out that Jean's nagging demands pushed him to drink. He did not want to take responsibility for his own decisions.

Even though Jean saw the seriousness of Tom's drinking bouts, she often drank with him. I began to talk with her about her own dependency on alcohol—which she refused to admit. After a year I suggested to both Jean and Tom that they stop drinking. They defensively banded together against the idea. I said, "As soon as you start drinking, you get disrespectful. I can see how wonderful it would be for both of you if you stopped drinking altogether."

Although Jean and Tom would not agree to stop drinking, I did get them to concede that they needed to keep the channels open between them by expressing their resentments as often as they surfaced. Furthermore, they agreed to do this only when they were not drinking.

After one of his alcohol "retreats" Tom announced he would stop drinking completely. He admitted that he felt out of control with alcohol and that he believed he was an alcoholic.

This was the beginning of a much-improved relationship. Tom's self-esteem improved immediately. He felt a burst of energy and enthusiasm that flowed into all areas of his life. Jean agreed not to drink around him, but she was reluctant to give up alcohol altogether. But soon she concluded that she too was an alcoholic, and she stopped drinking.

Without alcohol in the picture each of them found it less difficult to confront the other. As their commitment deepened they found it easier to catch themselves when old patterns resurfaced. After another year they had built enough trust that they were ready to be married.

Right before their wedding, however, Jean broke her no-drinking commitment. Tom, however, did not reject Jean or begin to drink himself. He confronted her, wanting her to talk to him about how she felt. "Each time I had a drink I felt bad about it, but then I'd want to do it again," she lamented. "I guess I'm afraid to be married. Sometimes I don't want to take responsibility."

Tom earnestly appealed to her. "Jean, I understand you're having a hard time, but I want you to talk to me about it rather than drinking. I'm committed to you, and together we can work out anything."

"If I open up to you, then I won't have an excuse for my drinking," she countered honestly.

Tom had clearly expressed to Jean what he wanted. Jean, in turn, was able to talk through her fears and resentments. With her recommitment to stop drinking Jean took a step toward maturity and responsibility. "This time," she declared, "I am doing this for me."

Although they were reluctant, a year later they did start to attend Alcoholics Anonymous meetings and realized that they were able to work through their alcohol problems. Although they were sober, their alcoholic character defects would take time to resolve.

Regulation 6: Be Brief: Limit All Fights to Five Minutes

A good fight is a brief fight, lasting five minutes or less.

If we are not able to put our point across in five minutes, we are not communicating well. Instead we may be attempting to win the fight, or we may be timidly beating around the bush. In any event, going on and on only leads to more upsetting and dissatisfied fighting.

Primarily, we must remember to say what we think. Secondarily, we must trust our power to influence each other by using a few strong, direct statements. We are not going to change the other person, but we will have an affect on them.

Peter and Beth: Endless Fighting. When Peter and Beth first came to see me, our therapy sessions were exhausting. After they started fighting, there was no stopping them. The minute they sat down they were off and running, verbally attacking each other. They were so intent on building their cases against each other that they talked at the same time, their voices becoming louder and louder.

It was obvious that they were not listening to each other, and in the bedlam I was unable to sort out what was being said. Actually, the picky details were really unimportant. What was important was the power struggle going on between them.

Beth, with a frantic look on her face, said, "Peter, you don't listen to me or care about what I need. You're always gone, and you never get to the things I'm asking you to do. I wanted you to finish fixing the table in the kitchen, but it is still propped up by bricks."

Peter impatiently interrupted by saying, "It would never be right for you. You are always asking for more, more, more. You always have twelve things on your list for me. I don't even want to get up in the morning. I'm sick and tired of trying to please you."

"*Please me?* That's a laugh," she countered. "You'd rather just talk to your friends. We haven't gone out alone for over a month."

"It's not much fun to be with you, that's for sure," he

agreed. "You are always criticizing me. No wonder I don't want to hang around. Besides, when it comes to helping get one of the house projects going—like pouring the concrete on the patio—you disappear. I told you I need your help!"

When they were engrossed in their arguing, Peter and Beth had little awareness of anything or anyone else. When I said that I wanted them to limit their fights to five minutes—and I repeated this statement often—they scarcely acknowledged they had heard me. I knew we would have to do some preliminary work before they would accept a five-minute fight.

In the first few weeks of therapy I continually expressed my frustration at their lack of respect for each other and for me. Actually, the basic lack of respect lay within themselves, and the central issue became their low self-esteem. Peter and Beth felt so poorly about themselves that the slightest negative feedback would trigger a fierce battle for survival. Each had to win to feel okay, so each had to put the other down to pull himself or herself up. They were so intent on being right and looking good that they were closed to each other's feelings. Consequently, little growth took place.

It became necessary for me to step back and tell myself that they were just fighting and not in a crisis. I needed to focus on the process occurring between them, not the content of their arguments, and to give them feedback on how they were interacting.

I reduced my expectations of what we could accomplish in a single session and began to think of doing just a little at a time. I insisted that they speak only to each other and not drag me in as a referee. I repeatedly made the point that their fights needed to end after five minutes. Even though my guideline seemed to fall on deaf ears, I know this point had an effect. I confined myself to applauding and booing their fight style, reinforcing the good efforts and pointing out the destructive moments.

Sometimes I was drawn into the uproar. But eventually

they began to realize that their fights affected them, and they had to live with the results. I could go home to peace and quiet, but they had to go home with each other. The most memorable occasion occurred on a day when they were getting more and more upset in a fight. I had warned them three times that they had gone beyond constructive bounds of fighting. They had almost totally disregarded my comments. I stood up and announced that the session was over. Their jaws dropped, and they pointed out that twenty minutes were left in the session. I stuck with my position, adding that I was charging them for the full hour as it was not my fault they had chosen to squander the time. Subdued, they quietly left.

In the next session both of them talked about the strong reaction they had to the short session. For the first time they had fully realized the futility of their behavior, and they felt embarrassed and ashamed.

"I can see how bad it gets when I'm trying to win," Peter admitted sheepishly.

"I want to start fighting better."Beth agreed. "I want to set the clock for five minutes and then stop fighting no matter what. But sometimes I get so caught up in the fight I get frantic."

"I can see that I do need to think more of what's important to you, Beth," Peter quietly stated. "I've been wanting my own way no matter what you think."

She smiled. "I know I ask too much of you. I think I feel helpless that you won't do anything, so I give you a big list."

He thought for a moment, then said, "I don't think it's the things we do that are so important. I want to feel that you care about me. Sometimes I feel like a machine instead of a person!

"You are special to me, Peter. I really had a good time with you Saturday night. It felt wonderful to go out by ourselves and talk." She gave him a hug.

With less tension, they began to listen to each other

rather than try to win or resolve their issues. From then on, when they began to get carried away in their fighting, a small reminder was all that was necessary. A new respect developed between them.

In summary, these six rules are required for fair fighting in all relationships:
1. Show Respect: For Self and Others
2. Maintain Equality: No Winners or Losers
3. Fight Safely: No Violence
4. Be Reasonable: No Hysterics
5. Be Clean and Sober: No Drugs
6. Be Brief: Limit All Fights to Five Minutes

Copy this list onto a card and hang it on the refrigerator for a constant reminder of what is necessary to make an argument constructive. If either person feels the fight was not good, go over the list the next day and discuss what could be improved. You will find you need to personalize your list by adding additional rules that apply to your individual fight problems.

Chapter Seven

Fighting Fair in the Clinches

"Therefore, as God's chosen people, holy and dearly loved, clothe yourselves with compassion, kindness, humility, gentleness and patience. Bear with each other and forgive whatever grievances you may have against one another. Forgive as the Lord forgave you."

Colossians 3:12, 13

This Scripture admonishes us not to harbor a grudge once an argument is concluded. After we've had our say we need to let go of the anger. When we start feeling the aftermath of hurt, we soften and can forgive each other. There is a lot to learn about good fighting. I have been teaching it for many years and constantly make new discoveries.

The six regulations for constructive fighting presented in Chapter 6 provide a solid foundation for the positive, healthy exchange of negative information. However, as you begin to practice these six basic rules in your relationship, a number of additional guidelines can help you apply the rules in particular situations. So let's continue discussing clean fighting with guidelines for the day-to-day clinches.

Guideline 1: Stay Until the End

It's important that both people hear each other out. Sometimes one wants to leave the fight because he or she is anxious. This couple will want to establish an agreement that they will stay in the room until both people have expressed themselves—or for a period of five minutes, whichever comes first. There must be an opportunity for mutual expression or both partners will feel frustrated. The one who expresses himself or herself will feel this way because no response has been received; the one who withdraws will feel tense because his or her feelings are still bottled up.

Sometimes, as in the following example, both people take turns withdrawing from a fight because they are so afraid. This makes complete communication impossible, so the problems mount.

Steve and Barbara: Taking Turns Fleeing. Steve and Barbara had a difficult time allowing themselves even a five-minute fight. They took turns acting tough, but underneath, each was very upset and afraid of the other's anger. On the nights when Steve gathered his courage to confront Barbara, she would withdraw to the bedroom, get into bed, pull the covers over her head and pretend she was asleep. Steve would stand beside the bed sputtering in frustration and would be awake off and on through the night feeling tense and restless. But Steve also withdrew when Barbara confronted him. He would go to the other room, then walk outside and finally drive around the block to get away.

Both of them saw the value of short fights to clear the air and get their relationship back to normal. But even though they believed this rationally, neither of them felt they could trust their anger. Each was afraid they'd lose control, and this frightening prospect caused them to run from each other when confronted.

During therapy I discovered that both Steve and Barbara had domineering mothers. Barbara's mother would bark out orders to the family. Early in life, Barbara, afraid of her mother's anger, decided to conform to her mother's wishes to get the cuddling she needed. Conforming to her mother's demands, however, was a poor substitute for feeling loved by her mother. Therefore, Barbara built up unspoken resentments which caused her to avoid her mother. Barbara needed to learn to give and receive love by allowing herself to be angry with the people who mattered most to her. Scary though it was, Barbara needed to take some risks by constructively confronting her mother.

Steve's mother frequently withdrew from him. She would go into the bedroom and read her days away. Being the oldest child, Steve was responsible for his younger brother and sister, a role he resented. After his mother and father divorced, Steve's mother pushed him into the role of husband substitute. Her demands on him were so great and the warmth she provided was so little that Steve eventually rebelled into wild, drunken sprees from which his mother often had to rescue him. Indirectly Steve had to go to great lengths to get the attention he craved from his mother.

Steve and Barbara also carried the insecurity of having been rejected by their fathers. Both their fathers divorced their mothers and only visited them infrequently during their childhood. So Barbara feared that if she fought with Steve, he would leave her as her father had left her mother.

Steve heard bad things about his dad from his mom. He saw his dad as weak, since he had an addiction to prescription drugs and was never able to stop using them. Steve had never said anything to his dad about this issue. His father died, and Steve's upset feelings brought him into therapy.

An important part of Steve and Barbara's therapy was learning to express their feelings of anger, hurt and warmth to their parents. Even though Steve's father was dead, Steve could express his feelings in my office by hitting the stump with a rolled-up magazine, talking to a pillow which represented his father and role-playing with other men in his group. He was mad his dad had deserted him by dying and that he had never shown Steve how to stand up to his mom. As Steve voiced his feelings he felt more like an adult. As he practiced expressing his feelings he felt equal to his father and thus gained masculine strength.

Barbara took small steps with her mom. She made phone calls and wrote letters, each time saying she wanted to be closer to her mom, see her more and have some talks. Then she got together with her for lunch, a walk on the beach or a cup of tea. Each time she said one thing from the past that had bothered her.

Finally they had a long talk about Barbara being afraid of her mom's bossiness. Her mother was surprised how upset Barbara became but was able to admit she had been too harsh. The balance of power shifted in this moment. They were able to feel strong together in that open time of confession and forgiveness. Barbara was able to see she had the same spunkiness her mom exhibited.

Understanding each other's past helped Steve and Barbara understand each other's fear of fighting. Feeling stronger with their parents helped them to be stronger with each other. They also learned to trust their love for each other and to accept criticism. They began to believe that they would not be judged or rejected by each other during confrontation.

They reached the point where they could make and keep the commitment to stay and fight for five minutes. Sometimes they still felt like fleeing the fight, but instead they designated areas in the house to which each could retreat *after* the fight. Their new guideline helped bring calmness, respect and team effort to their relationship.

Guideline 2: Disagree Daily

Every day we have angry feelings. Some are minor and some bother us a lot. If we find we are storing up resentments and exploding on a weekly or monthly basis, we need to commit ourselves to talk daily for 15 minutes, to share what we liked or did not like about our relationship that day. That short amount of time can be surprisingly satisfying. When we are current with our feelings, we don't become tense. Setting a time to discuss feelings establishes a healthy new pattern for dealing with resentments. Each day we know we have time reserved, and thus permission granted, to take care of our feelings.

Jon and Chris: Playing Hard to Get. Jon and Chris were very good at maintaining a calm, cool, unruffled facade around each other. If something in the relationship bothered either of them, they swallowed it in silence instead of discussing it. They were afraid of closeness, so they seized their dislikes as ammunition for silently punishing each other and maintaining a comfortable distance.

But the quieter they became with each other on the outside, the stormier their anger raged inside until one of them exploded—usually Jon was provoked by Chris. She would disrupt the pattern of silence by coming after him to see what was bothering him. All she had to do was poke at him a little, and he would erupt in a frightening rage and deliver a bitter tongue-lashing. But instead of expressing her own anger in return, Chris defended herself with tears and a pathetic face whenever Jon attacked. Jon had learned to ignore Chris' emotional tactics.

After the initial explosion the emotional stalemate between Jon, who was cold and biting, and Chris, who felt sorry for herself, would last for days. Finally Jon would lower his guard and begin talking about what was really bothering him. Jon's openness would encourage Chris to express some of her anger strongly and directly. Finally peace was restored to their relationship, and their calm exteriors were reset until the next storm boiled to the surface in a hurtful explosion.

Jon and Chris didn't like their pattern of expressing anger. They wanted to be able to respond faster to the warning signs, so they came to me for therapy. From the outset I stressed the necessity of their talking to each other daily about their feelings instead of playing guessing games. They needed to short-circuit the days of accumulating and withholding anger.

Hitting the stump a number of times in my office helped loosen them up and acquaint them with their anger so that it did not seem so frightening to them. This experience launched them into a commitment to talk daily for 15 minutes about their feelings.

Sometimes they were faithful to their commitment, and sometimes they drifted back into their old, uncomfortable pattern. It took time for them to feel successful in their assignment. They complained they couldn't think of anything to say; one of them fell silent while the other said too much; they forgot to talk; they went on for an hour and burned out. One by one we talked through the obstacles. As they improved their ability to express anger constructively, they liked it more.

Eventually, when they followed through with their daily talks, they were able to confront their anger, state their hurts and move into warmth together on a daily basis. As they experienced positive results from daily disagreements, they were more open to continue them. Their goal was to share more of themselves with each other and to become best friends. Their meaningful, daily talks from the heart helped them move toward their goals.

Guideline 3: Balance Your Participation

No one likes to be bullied! If one partner dominates the fighting, each may need to make a commitment to find a more satisfactory balance. The quieter partner needs to be stronger by shouting back and making firmer statements to defend himself or herself. And the noisier partner needs to lower his or her voice and listen more to the other person.

Without equal participation in the fight, both people go away frustrated. The passive partner feels bottled up inside, and such pent-up emotion causes trouble later. The aggressive person feels rejected by the lack of response from the passive partner. This person gets even "pushier" in an attempt to elicit some information.

Both partners need to participate in the fight for it to work well. Ideally, we go back and forth in our short angry statements. But achieving such a balanced exchange requires courage, commitment and discipline.

Tom and Amy: Withholding and Exploding. Tom and Amy came to me in a crisis. They were having difficulty fighting in a fair, equal exchange. Their last fight had ended in a raucous blow-up which caused the neighbors to complain. Amy accused Tom of being a bully, and she was afraid he might hurt her. Tom didn't accept that he was intimidating. He blamed Amy for goading him into losing control. He complained that she kept after him until he could not stand her nagging anymore.

In their last fight Amy had come home from work in a grouchy mood and complained to Tom about her day. Tom avoided her by burying his head in the newspaper. She berated him for ignoring her, and when he still replied tersely and coldly she became hysterical. Finally she moved closer to him, screaming uncontrollably, and Tom exploded and shoved her away.

As I listened to them tell the story, I noted how Tom kept himself under control. His face was expressionless, and his words were clearly and slowly enunciated. If Amy attempted to interrupt his measured sentences, Tom would silence her by raising his eyebrows and his voice. Amy, on the other hand, was visibly upset. Her voice was quick to rise with the sound of panic. She spoke to Tom in a pleading voice, obviously seeking reassurance from him.

Both Tom and Amy came from insecure homes and felt unloved. As a boy Tom had left his family home early and had missed out on some nurturing he needed. Amy had been beaten by her father while her terrified mother watched. Also, Amy's little brother was the favorite. Amy's parents doted over him so Amy often felt left out.

I had individual sessions with Tom and Amy in which I raised their self-esteem by focusing on the positive aspects of their personalities. I reminded them that God loves them and delights in them. I emphasized the need for them to like themselves first so they didn't strain their relationship. Otherwise they would blame the other person for their own bad feelings. I pointed out that they competed for love and acceptance by putting each other down. Instead they needed to adopt a positive approach by being friendly and asking for support. I told them, "You will get back exactly what you give. If you love and praise the other you will be loved and praised in return."

In their fighting, Tom and Amy had to work for a balance in their expression. The critical moment in their unproductive pattern was when Amy raised her voice and expressed herself clearly to Tom. If she did not get a response from him she would become hysterical in a desperate attempt to make Tom react. I suggested that Tom also raise his voice at that critical moment as a way of being involved with Amy in the fight. He was extremely reluctant to "stoop to her level," stating his preference for being more rational and mature. Finally Tom admitted that if he dropped his composed manner and matched Amy's emotional expression he would lose the upper hand in the relationship.

More important than the need to control the relationship, Tom needed to control his own anger. His appearance of control was only a mask hiding his fear of explosive outbursts. I spent time helping Tom feel safe about exploring his anger within prescribed limits on a daily basis. I explained that he must express his anger as it comes up so it will not build into a problem. Raising his voice could equalize the relationship so that neither of them would need to escalate the battle. Explosions only occur when power in a relationship is lop-sided.

Tom had difficulty relinquishing control of his voice. At first I had him and Amy stand across the room from each other to practice projecting their voices. It was just as important for Amy to practice as for Tom. She had to learn to avoid panicking in a fight and screaming hysterically.

By practicing with Amy in my office and in a group session, and by arguing successfully at home a few times, Tom gradually built some confidence. He was willing to stand up for himself in a firm and genuinely angry tone of voice.

Guideline 4: Drop Grudges

Holding grudges gives fighting a bad name! In a constructive fight it is important for both people to drop the issue once the feelings have been expressed. We can even resume normal conversation and activities with each other. If we hold onto our anger, it hardens into bitterness and coldness. We're trying to win the argument and control the other person by clinging to feelings which should have been resolved in the five-minute fight. Too much time for enjoying companionship gets wasted by grudge-punishing.

I used to think I was making my point in my arguments more emphatic when I was silent and cold. I thought Jack would wither with my dirty looks. But the opposite is true. The more I hold onto the issue, the easier it is for my husband to forget what the argument is about and be angry with me for holding onto the anger! My point is lost, and I become the problem.

Guy and Paula: "Dirty Looks." Guy and Paula came to me because their fights were ending in stand-offs that drug on for days and weeks. The problems in their relationship were rooted in the poor self-concept each of them held.

While growing up, Paula developed the reputation for being a trouble-maker in her family. She did not finish high school and drifted through several years of heavy drug use. She felt guilty about the harm she had done to her family. When we met, Paula was still adjusting to being a wife and the mother of a six-month-old son. She usually managed to keep her home attractive and running smoothly. She was particularly devoted to her son and cared for him tenderly. But her past haunted her, and she had difficulty giving herself credit for the good things she did. When I commented on her accomplishments, she quickly pointed out that she had not done the dishes for almost a week and that she had too much to drink the night before.

Guy also had an extremely low opinion of himself. As a child he had been repeatedly spanked by his father, so he had trouble feeling okay about himself. Now at age 27, he had gone from job to job and did not feel successful. Money was a constant struggle, as he found himself living from paycheck to paycheck. He was so timid that when Paula complained, tears sprang from his eyes instead of angry words from his lips.

Since both Guy and Paula felt personally weak, it was not easy for them to fight with each other. Guy alternated between trying to please Paula—keeping her from being angry with him—to being high-handed and intimidating—bullying her as his father had bullied him. Paula did not feel strong enough to respond openly and directly, so when she got up-tight, she became close-mouthed. She would give Guy a dirty look and withdraw into a long and silent coldness.

Once Paula withdrew Guy could not budge her to interact with him. His heart sank as he realized he might be snubbed for days. She would not talk to him or do things with him no matter how he cajoled. By the end of a week they were both exhausted. A fight represented alienation to Guy, so once Paula "thawed" he returned to his usual pattern of avoiding conflict. But problems would eventually build to an explosion and again produce days of painful silence.

I encouraged Guy and Paula to establish some rules to help them feel safe enough to air their grievances and break the pattern of grudge-holding which was suffocating their relationship. They were afraid that their arguments would erupt into physical violence, so they made a nonviolence agreement. Then they were ready to move to the next step of agreeing to drop the fight when it was over. They talked at length about letting go of the fight within an hour after it had ended, allowing themselves time to feel hurt and let the words sink in. They agreed that at the end of the hour they would speak to each other to avoid hanging onto a disagreement to punish each other or to get the upper hand.

Finally they were ready to commit themselves to resume normal living with each other within an hour after the fighting. The goal was to pick up where they left off before the fight: fixing lunch, watching TV or whatever was happening. To succeed at their commitment they needed to trust that the words exchanged during the fight would be seriously considered by the other, making a prolonged grudge unnecessary.

The quality of their days became amazingly better. They could relax and enjoy each other. Instead of days of coldness they had one hour of arguing and distress, and the rest of the time they were feeling good. Their sense of humor was restored, and sessions became fun.

Guideline 5: Don't Make Threats

Threats to leave each other uttered during fights undermine healthy relationships. All of us fear the pain of rejection. Threats are usually power plays we use when we don't feel strong, want to be in control and do not want to feel hurt. But in order to give deeply of ourselves in an emotional exchange, we each need the assurance that our partner will not desert us—or threaten to desert us. Knowing that the foundation of the relationship is solid gives us the courage to be more open, honest and vulnerable. Making a commitment to abolish all threats during fighting establishes this foundation.

Bob and Susan: Breaking Up and Breaking Up. Bob and Susan had been together for ten years and had broken up ten times. When they first came to see me, they were talking about breaking up again. When the going got tough between them, they both withdrew. One of them would suggest that the relationship was over, and the other one, to avoid showing hurt, would agree.

Although they reacted to emotional stress the same way, their backgrounds were very different. Susan was the only child in an old-fashioned, old world family. She complained that her upbringing was lonely, quiet and gloomy, lacking excitement or emotion. Susan felt embarrassed because her parents were plain and dull, and she learned to ignore them by entertaining herself in her own world. She became a master at rising above unpleasant situations and raising her tolerance level which caused her to become oblivious to her own needs and discomfort.

Bob was the eldest of five children, often responsible for his younger siblings. He did not receive enough attention or love from his parents. When he felt ignored he would withdraw to rest and lick his wounds. He learned to be solitary and to take care of himself.

Both Bob and Susan learned early to cover up their feelings and keep people at a distance to avoid being hurt. They each developed stubborn strength and pride as children to survive in families where personal contact was missing. As adults they continued this defensive pattern to assure comfort in relationships.

At the beginning of therapy Bob and Susan resisted my suggestion that they declare a moratorium on giving up on each other. Sometimes their arguments about no longer caring for one another were so good they almost convinced me. But seeing me begin to weaken brought them to their senses, and they took more responsibility for cooperating.

I pointed out to them that any sign of deep emotion between them caused them to panic and, in their desire to control the situation, to make outrageous statements. During a rather emotional time together, we were able to identify and discuss several of the irrational statements of rejection they used, such as:

- I never was attracted to you;
- I never have enjoyed people; I'm perfectly happy alone;
- I never wanted to get married in the first place;
- We don't have enough in common with each other to have a good relationship;
- I'm working on myself, not the relationship, and your opinions don't matter to me;
- It's over; I don't have any feelings left for you.

Bob and Susan had six major eruptions during their first year of therapy with me. They took turns calling off the relationship. At each break my heart sank. The one calling it off would come in for a session with the other but would sit by stubbornly and coldly. I would attempt unsuccessfully to get a good argument going. One partner got angry while the other claimed that the relationship was over and that he/she did not even feel any anger. Toward the end of each session some mutual sparks would fly and the stubborn partner would begin to come around.

During one of our more rational sessions I was able to convince Bob and Susan that they must drop all threats of leaving the relationship. I pointed out that I saw their threats as cover-ups for underlying issues which they could avoid bringing up by simply threatening to give up. I suggested that by dropping this disruptive pattern there would be a chance for something more positive to happen between them.

Meanwhile they could put their hand in Jesus' hand and trust that he would watch over and bless their marriage. We prayed together, and they cried. They gave up the struggle to control each other.

They finally made a commitment to talk about issues instead of threatening each other with break-ups. They discovered that, without their favorite weapon, they were stuck with each other. Since they had eliminated the option of separation, they were forced to work on their relationship. In a few months they began sharing aloud their frustrations and disappointments with each other. Some very constructive fights occurred between them, and, because they cared about each other, they began to bend in each other's direction. Most of all, they felt safe with each other—secure that they loved each other and would not leave each other, even when they were angry. They enjoyed the new freedom that resulted from resolving to stay together.

Guideline 6: Blend Thoughts and Feelings

Constructive fighting requires the blending of the head (thoughts) and the heart (feelings). Once our feelings have been considered, our intellect should make the final decisions. Our feelings tell us clearly what we want and what bothers us, while our thoughts show us the best way to achieve what is good for us. We would be out of balance in a fight without both elements. If one or both partners only express thoughts in a fight, they run the risk of overloading the argument with facts, case-building and analysis. On the other hand, if one or both partners only express feelings, they run the risk of overloading the argument with temper tantrums and hysterics.

Mat and Louise: Rhetoric and Hysteria. Mat did not like nor trust his feelings, and he used his intellect to control them. When he first came to see me he was in the process of separating from his first wife. He was obviously upset and struggling to suppress his anger and hurt. He wanted me to see his side—and only his side—of the story.

Mat immediately impressed me as a powerful man who would brook no interference with his plans. I was not surprised to learn that he was the senior partner in a law firm. He was used to getting his way, and he had the verbal ability to turn events in the direction he desired.

Mat viewed fighting as a debate to be won by the quickest, sharpest, most ruthless adversary. He would pounce on his opponents, interrupt them, raise his voice, become sarcastic and threaten to walk out. His fighting technique consisted of sentence after sentence of clever rhetoric and argument. But underneath this facade Mat was yearning to be loved and appreciated. I could feel his loneliness and inner struggle as he worked so hard to impress others with his intellect.

Mat was in fact a very lonely, insecure man who was unwilling to lower his guard because of an enormous amount of hurt hiding behind it. Thoughts and words were his protection. He carefully analyzed and logically explained everything. He told well-documented stories designed to blame others for his problems. When I brought him to the stump to get him to work on his feelings he merely talked faster.

Sometimes I got through to him, and Mat would become belligerent and express his anger by shouting. A few times he stormed out of the office. At one point he did not come back for three weeks. But somehow he realized that, painful though it was, his anger needed to be confronted. So he kept coming back, bravely working to open himself emotionally. Over the next few years Mat worked on asking for what he wanted instead of demanding it.

During this time Mat married Louise. It was immediately obvious that Mat had met someone who would stand up to him. She was also used to having her own way, but her method of gaining control was to overreact emotionally. When Mat built a verbal case and turned the issues back on her, Louise would match wits with him until she realized he was getting the best of her. Then she would literally stamp her feet and scream hysterically. When Mat realized that her emotionalism was drowning his argument, he exploded with icy threats.

Though their exchanges did bring their emotions to the surface, the gains were outweighed by a hurtful loss of respect and trust. Both of them needed to work on giving up control and being more direct about what they wanted. Each needed to blend thoughts and feelings so they could fight on equal ground all the time.

After practicing good, balanced fighting, Mat and Louise each found confidence in their power and influence over the other and began to relax. We were able to work on their low self-esteem and fears of inadequacy and rejection which stemmed from poor family backgrounds. I stressed repeatedly that they were both irreplaceable; that each of them was a strong, unique individual.

In time they realized that was so. They were able to appreciate each other without fearing their loss of identity. Today Mat and Louise are a dynamic couple, strong parents and active in the community. Their success illustrates that good relationships don't just happen. We have to roll up our sleeves and work on them.

Guideline 7: Add Your Own Fight Rules

After you have some experience with arguing in your closest relationships, stop to evaluate how you are doing based on the rules in Chapter 6 and the guidelines discussed in this chapter. You may need to add some new guidelines which we have not covered. It is important to tailor your fighting to meet your own particular fears and needs.

Critique your fights often. Sometimes after a bad fight you don't want to talk about *why* the experience was destructive instead of constructive. You are afraid that if you resurrect the memory of the bad fight you will have a bad experience again. But it is important to push through this fear to talk about what went wrong. If a bad fight starts up again, back off and try again later. At this point the content of the fight is not as important as the rules you are using (or misusing). You must get past the content to talk about how the fight was conducted and to correct the misconduct.

Each couple must enter into constructive fighting by agreeing together on basic ground rules for safety. The regulations and guidelines presented here are an excellent starting place. Then you can decide on particular commitments which pertain to your own individual needs. These personal guidelines will help you focus on your specific problems and give you tools for fixing the trouble spots. Each couple I work with has a steadily evolving list of formal and informal rules for constructive fighting which are designed especially by and for them.

The rules you make, however, are not to be used as ammunition against each other. Rather, partners are encouraged to become teammates in creating a safe environment in which they can let their hair down through confrontation. All of us are afraid of arguing to some extent, and we all need some tools to rely on for security in fighting.

As couples become more aware of what they are doing, they are able to add new tools to their "tool kits." No two couples are alike; each has its own special needs for expressing anger, and each must develop its own special ways of dealing with anger constructively. Each couple must create a list of guidelines, then discuss, accept and post it where it can be seen frequently.

Chapter Eight

Discover Your Unexpressed Anger

"For you were once in darkness, but now you are
light in the Lord. Live as children of light (for the fruit
of light consists in all goodness, righteousness and
truth) and find out what pleases the Lord."
Ephesians 5:8-10

To live as children of the light and to do what pleases our Father, let us picture Jesus standing by our side as we express our anger. Sometimes I imagine Jesus' face superimposed over my husband's to help me remain respectful with my communication. Jesus has told us that what we do to our brothers and sisters we do to him.

You have been reading about the value of expressing anger, how to do it and how not to do it. Now it's time to take some specific action to express some of your withheld anger. You will need to muster your courage to go forward, and here are some suggestions to help you get started.

Take Time to Focus on Your Feelings

The critical first step is to identify the unexpressed anger which is trapped inside you. Sometimes you won't notice it unless you specifically look for it. To be aware of what is bothering you, set aside some time each day—a few minutes in the morning and again at night—to examine your feelings. You might utilize some uninterrupted moments while driving, jogging, brushing your teeth, eating lunch or sitting quietly. Select the time that is best for you.

Plan to do this faithfully every day for one month to build it into a habit. When this process becomes habitual you will be more aware of your feelings and will handle them as they occur. You will no longer have to schedule time to look for them.

Once you have selected a daily time, ask yourself four penetrating questions to pinpoint any unexpressed feelings: (1) What is bothering me? (2) Who am I angry with? (3) What did I say? (4) What do I need to say? If after several moments of thought you can honestly admit that nothing or no one is bothering you, your evaluation period is complete. Most of the time, however, some bothersome people and situations will come to mind. Thoughtfully work through the following three steps:

1. Identify your unfinished business. If the four questions reveal some unfinished business in your relationships, jot down a few notes describing the situations which must be confronted in terms of what you must say or do to clear the air. Choose situations you are stewing about.

Rate each issue of unfinished business according to its difficulty on a scale of one (easiest) to five (hardest). The ratings may describe the difficulty of the relationship and/or the difficulty of the nature of confrontation. Note the sample list below—five items representing five levels of difficulty:

• Tell the gardener that I don't think he's been putting in the hours he's charging me for (Difficulty: 1).

• Tell my friend that I want to talk more meaningfully about ourselves rather than just chatting (Difficulty: 2).

• Tell my office manager that I want him to do a more careful job with my appointment book (Difficulty: 3).

• Tell my cousin I need her caring and involvement rather than her advice about my teenager (Difficulty: 4).

• Tell my husband that I resent that he doesn't take into account what I want to spend money on (trips and furniture), while he is eager to spend money on what he thinks is important (investments) (Difficulty: 5).

2. Make plans for confrontation. Decide when and where you are going to confront these people. You will be tempted to put off confrontations. But keep in mind that the sooner you talk to them, the better you will feel. Keep the list where you will see it often and check off each situation when you face it. You may want to jot down three or four situations you would like to handle during the week and carry your list around with you as a reminder. Even when you are not directly thinking about them, you will be subconsciously working on what you're going to do.

You will find it helpful to share the details of your list with a few trusted friends. Tell them what happened and what you're going to say. They will probably be interested and glad to give you feedback. You will also profit from hearing yourself rehearse your strategy aloud.

3. Evaluate each encounter. After you have completed a confrontation and checked it off your list, take time to evaluate what happened. How did you feel as you handled each situation? Write down your feelings, as illustrated below with the sample confrontations, to help you stay focused on them

• Tell the gardener that I don't think he's been putting in the hours he's charging me for (Difficulty: 1). *I feel good that he acknowledged his failure and that he will charge me less.*

• Tell my friend that I want to talk more meaningfully about ourselves rather than just chatting (Difficulty: 2). *I feel good that we have already started doing it!*

• Tell my office manager that I want him to do a more careful job with my appointment book (Difficulty: 3). *I feel frustrated that he made a big deal out of my request and threatened to quit.*

• Tell my cousin I need her caring and involvement rather than her advice about my teenager (Difficulty: 4). *I feel excited that we were able to have a good, quiet discussion.*

• Tell my husband that I resent that he doesn't take into account what I want to spend money on (trips and furniture), while he is eager to spend money on what he thinks is important (investments) (Difficulty: 5). *I am glad that I spoke up. Though we did argue, I can feel progress toward planning our spending together.*

Expressing anger to others in this way is a learning process. If your confrontation is upsetting, it's okay to feel sad or hurt about it. Just as we limit a fight to five minutes, so we must limit our self-criticism to five minutes. Admit to yourself what you did wrong , but don't keep on scolding yourself. After five minutes of learning from your mistake, you need to decide what to do next.

One exciting aspect of communication is that it is fluid— you can change what you have said. You can go back to someone and say, "I feel upset that I went on and on, overstating my point," or "I think I sounded like I was rejecting you, and I didn't mean that."

Be sure to listen to the other person. Encourage him or her to give you feedback, too. If the confrontation is only one-sided, the quiet person will build up resentments. We want to have arguments that are "an *exchange* of negative information."

In dealing with unfinished business we stand to lose the most with people who are the closest to us. We need them, and their rejection would hurt us deeply. Since we risk more in confronting our intimate relationships, we may be more fearful to approach them with our feelings. Therefore, I encourage you to start by working on the items you have rated with lower numbers. They are the easiest to deal with; accomplishing them will build your confidence for the more difficult confrontations.

Of course, situations will come up daily in all five levels of relationships, and you will have to handle them. But for starters, channel your main energies toward your acquaintances for several weeks. Practice in this area paves the way for stepping into more difficult areas. Just remember to always be genuine; don't make something up for the sake of practice. Also, be careful not to take out major anger on a minor situation.

Confronting Acquaintances

Usually your easiest interactions will take place with casual acquaintances. In this category you might include people to whom you only say "hello" or speak a few sentences occasionally. This group includes the people who serve us (insurance agent, store clerk, postman, etc.) and people we serve (customers or clients). Even these simple interactions can easily create conflicts in which we need to say what we think and feel.

For example, Mary noticed that her yard, which she paid Harry, the gardener, to tend, was looking messier than usual. The ivy was hanging over the curb and growing into the agapanthus beds. The trees needed pruning and many plants needed fertilizer. For what she paid Harry she thought she was entitled to have her yard look neat and tidy. Besides, he had kept it well for eight months, so why was he slipping up now? She jotted down the unfinished business she needed to pursue with Harry: *Tell the gardener that I don't think he's been putting in the hours he's charging me for.*

Next, she needed to decide what she was going to do and say about the problem. She decided to persist in calling Harry (he is often hard to reach) so he would know that the issue was important to her. She wanted to tell him clearly what was bothering her without overreacting or being too harsh. She also wanted to give him some positive feedback on what he did do well. Their phone conversation went like this:

Mary: Harry, I've been wanting to talk to you about the garden.

Harry: I don't get to see you when I'm there on Fridays.

Mary: That's true, and I think we need to talk from time to time so I can give you feedback about what I want done and to compliment you on the special work you have done.

Harry: I'm not always sure what's important to you.

Mary: Most important to me is that the yard looks neat and trim. Recently, you have not kept it up as well as in past months. It seems you're not putting in the same number of hours.

Harry: I've had trouble with one of my men—he's been out sick—and I'm behind on another big job. I didn't work as many hours on your yard as I was supposed to, and your bill will be less this month.

Mary: I'm glad to hear that. I only wish you had told me sooner. If you had notified me about your problem I would have been understanding instead of resentful.

Harry: I kept thinking I would catch up. I guess I should have called.

Mary: Are you sure you want to continue our maintenance? I'm afraid you'll get busy again and our place will suffer.

Harry: I want to do your place, and I am arranging my schedule so it won't happen again.

Mary: I'm glad. You do an excellent job, you're artistic, and you're fast. I like having you as our gardener. Also, I'll plan to be home once a month when you're doing your work so we can talk in person for a few minutes.

Her conversation with Harry was easy. She started out gradually instead of jumping on him. He sounded relieved to admit his failure, and when he did they were free to recommit to one another. She also listened to his needs and learned that he missed the personal contact with her.

By the end of the conversation, there was a good balance

between confrontation and support. Their communication definitely improved their relationship and opened the way for future positive discussions.

Confronting Casual Friends

Under this heading are people we enjoy sharing time with occasionally: a jogging partner, someone you meet for lunch once a month and so forth. They are not the intimate friends with whom we share the most personal items of our lives. Still, our casual friends are sources of fun and companionship, and we talk with them about some of the events in our lives and the feelings which are appropriate to this level.

Barbara's relationship with Helen is an example of a casual friendship. But Barbara had a problem with Helen. The last few times they were together Barbara felt restless because Helen talked on and on about her two kids and all the details of her PTA project. Barbara was bothered that Helen talked only about events and not about her feelings. Barbara didn't need to hear Helen's deepest feelings, but she did want to know whether Helen felt satisfied, enthused, frustrated or unappreciated.

Furthermore, Barbara found herself talking with Helen about her kids, the new furniture and her social events instead of how *she* was feeling. She came away from these conversations feeling dissatisfied. Barbara summarized her unfinished business with the words: *Tell my friend that I want to talk more meaningfully about ourselves rather than just chat.*

Barbara decided that she needed to initiate more conversation from the heart with Helen. To start, she phoned Helen to tell her about her thoughts and feelings on the issue:

Barbara: Helen, I've been wanting you to tell me more about yourself instead of so much about your PTA project.

Helen: Well, my PTA work is important to me.

Barbara: I know, but I am interested to know more about

you too. I know I also need to share more of my feelings with you, so you'll be comfortable sharing with me.

Helen: Well, that's the way I am. I wish you'd accept me the way I am.

Barbara: I like you a lot, Helen, and I would feel even closer to you if you shared more from your heart. What I'd like to share is that I've been feeling tired since I was sick a few weeks ago, and my work has been extra hard ever since. I'm not caught up yet; it's a strain.

Helen: I can imagine it's been hard. Your work sits waiting for you to come back. I've been worrying about my sister. She's been lonely since her divorce. She doesn't talk much about it. When I call her she sounds so cheerful. I wish she'd talk about it instead of sounding so brave.

Although Helen resented Barbara's confrontation at first, she joined in when Barbara shared about herself. Barbara felt good that they actually shared feelings in their first conversation after she raised the issue. It's important for us to take responsibility for talking on the level we desire others to talk on.

In casual friendships we don't need to elaborate on all the details about our problems and feelings. Yet we can at least communicate some of our feelings about the events we discuss. Furthermore, we will feel better if we express ourselves on a feeling level. How can we believe we are lovable if we never give others the chance to know us and love us by revealing some of our feelings to them?

Confronting Fellow Workers

This category includes those who work with us everyday: superiors, subordinates and peers. There is a great opportunity for expression in these relationships since they are close and continuous. And we must get along with these people because our livelihood depends on it. Even though we don't usually share the intimate details of our lives with our co-workers, these people are familiar to us and important to us.

Interaction with co-workers is often scarier than with casual friends because we can't walk away from work relationships. If a casual friend rejects our confrontations we can live with it more easily because we don't see him or her everyday. But if the person at the next desk rejects us, we must live with the possible hurt and anger every working day. Yet if we confront co-workers well, the result can be improved teamwork and increased loyalty that will be a source of great joy and productivity for everyone on the staff.

When confronting a co-worker, approach him or her respectfully with an attitude of working out the problems. When confronting negative work habits, always give some positive feedback about the person's work to keep a balanced perspective. Then make your point and drop it; don't keep hammering on the issue.

Ann, a beautician who owns her own salon, was dependent upon Bob to keep the front desk running smoothly while she was in the back with her customers. Bob had been careless in his handling of the appointment book, making some errors which had lost some customers. But Bob had difficulty accepting criticism, and Ann was often afraid to confront him because he remained upset for days. Each time she approached him with a correction she realized that he might leave. Yet she made a decision to confront him: *Tell my office manager that I want him to do a more careful job with my appointment book.*

Ann carefully planned her strategy for the confrontation. She selected a time when neither of them was feeling pressure. She would not pounce on him harshly but would begin by giving him credit for the work he *was* doing well. Their conversation went as follows:

Ann: Bob, I've been feeling good about your accuracy with the ledger cards and summary sheets. You have learned to balance the two to the penny, and it seems to be getting easier for you.

Bob: I feel good about that also, even though I get a little frustrated sometimes when I can't find an error.

Ann: I want you to concentrate more of your efforts on the appointment book. There have been a few discrepancies lately.

Bob: I've seen you make errors in it also. I think you are a little picky about it.

Ann: If I make errors, I want them pointed out to me. We all need to improve. We had two customers show up at the same time last week. I want to make sure it doesn't happen again.

Bob: I thought I was doing a good job, and now I feel hopeless about it. I'll never be able to do it well enough to please you.

Ann: I have noticed improvement, and I'm happy with your work. This is only one small area which needs improvement.

Bob: I'm not sure I should stay on.

Ann: Bob, I'd like you to be able to accept criticism without threatening to leave. I want you here. Your threats are disrespectful to both of us. I don't want to go on and on about this. Let's drop it for now and talk about it again later.

Ann was upset that Bob again threatened to quit, but she felt good about stating what bothered her and asking for what she wanted. Knowing Bob, she was confident that he would calm down, think over what Ann said and use the information she gave him. She could see that with practice these talks would get easier. Bob had improved since the last time she confronted him. She knew they'd need to follow up with another talk in a day or two.

Confronting Family Members

It is especially scary to confront family members because

these relationships are permanent. We cannot trade our relatives in for new models if we are not happy with them. They need us and we need them. Family roots give us a foundation of security, but they also create more potential for fear of rejection. Many of us have suffered from feeling like the black sheep of our family. Yet the benefits of open communication with family members greatly outweigh the risks. If we can feel at home in these confrontations, we will feel accepted and good about ourselves. Then we will bring these good feelings into other relationships.

We must take small steps when confronting the members of our families, dealing with only one issue at a time. We don't want to overwhelm and alienate them. It's important to develop a positive way of talking with them before attempting confrontation.

For example, Susan stays in touch with her older cousin, Betty. They send letters three or four times a year, talk on the phone every six weeks and occasionally drive to "meet in the middle" for lunch. They clearly like and respect each other.

Usually they have a relaxed good time, but Susan became upset with her older cousin because she felt Betty was being critical of the way she raised her son John. Betty acted superior to Susan which made Susan feel inadequate. Betty didn't say anything directly, but she sent Susan some articles which Susan took as a jab. So Susan decided to do something about the situation: *Tell my cousin I need her caring and involvement rather than her advice about my teenager.*

Susan decided that she needed to talk directly to Betty and bring her feelings out into the open. But she needed to be careful not to be judgmental about Betty being judgmental!

Susan: Betty, I appreciate your note and the articles on drugs that you sent. I know you mean well, but I don't believe that John's problems stem from marijuana.

Betty: The description sounds so much like him.

Susan: I believe John is upset about what to do with his life. He hasn't been able to settle down to school or a job. He's also upset with his girlfriend. That's why he's so moody.

Betty: I hope you'll read the book I sent you anyway.

Susan: Because you are my older cousin, I still feel like I'm blowing it when you give me advice. I remember many times when you worried about me getting into trouble. I really don't need you to take care of me anymore. I'm a responsible person, and I work hard at being a good mom. I just want your reaction—your opinions and feelings.

Betty: I know you can handle things. I got upset about John and wanted to help. I love you, Susan, though I don't always agree with what you're doing.

Susan: I've sensed that you don't approve, but you've never come out and said it. It would feel better if you said directly what is bothering you rather than beating around the bush.

Betty: O.K. I think you and Paul have not been strict enough with John, and you give him too much money.

Susan: I do have a hard time drawing guidelines for him. Paul and I don't agree sometimes. I'm afraid he'll be too hard on John. I'm too easy about the money because I hate to have John mad at me. I get scared he'll leave and never come back. Sometimes, Betty, you make things sound easy. It's not easy for me when I'm living in the situation.

Betty: I think you need to call more often when you feel scared, and I'll tell you that you are doing the right thing! John may not like you now but in the long run he'll love you. Our main job is to help our kids have good values as they go out into the world. I don't feel critical as much as helpful. I don't think I ever told you everything that I went through with Lance. Let me tell you now.

Susan's confrontation with Betty opened up a new dimension in their relationship. They both received much more than either of them imagined was possible. Susan never knew how much Betty cared. She had thought Betty was putting her down, but she wasn't. Betty was more willing to discuss her feelings than Susan had realized. Susan was able to get much needed support. Betty felt good to share *her* solitary burden of her trials with Lance. Both women benefitted from Susan's honest communication. Letting their hair down with each other brought them closer.

Confronting Intimate Relationships

God calls the majority of us to his sacred institution of marriage. He wants us to have the blessing of deep love which reflects his love for us. We are to love God with our whole heart. The husband is designated the head of the household, and he is to love his wife as he would love his own body. The wife is to submit to her husband with love and respect.

We are not created to be islands. Most of us reach out for the deep caring of an intimate relationship with another person. We need the companionship, the support, the cuddling and the sex which only a monogamous, committed marriage offers. We need someone who cares for us almost as deeply as we care for ourselves. And we need to care about someone else in the same way.

Sometimes, even though you desire an intimate relationship, it may elude you or, having once been enjoyed, it may be lost to you through divorce or death. If you are single, you also need supportive, committed relationships with people who know you well and communicate with you deeply. Though the principles in this section apply specifically to marriage relationships, they can be adapted to close non-marital friendships.

One of the best ways to keep anger from building up in your intimate relationship is to schedule 15 uninterrupted minutes each day to sit down and talk with your partner. You will want to discuss what you like about your relationship

146 / The Gift of Anger

and what bothers you. A daily, uninterrupted 15-minute get-together, when you can communicate eye to eye and heart to heart, will prevent little complaints from building into large campaigns. Here's an example of how a daily 15-minute talk might sound:

He: At last, a chance to be with you. It's hectic when we first get home.

She: You're not kidding. Boy, do I need this time alone with you. I'd love to run away with you and play hooky.

He: We'll get a chance to have some fun this weekend. It's been a long, hard day for me. I had a few emergency appointments and only a half hour for lunch.

She: Sounds like a lot of stress. I had a normal sort of day, but I feel tired from just being in the office for 10 hours. My throat is scratchy too, and that bothers me.

He: I noticed you were grouchy this morning. I felt like you were ready to jump on me.

She: Yeah, I was grouchy. I'm not getting enough sleep. But sometimes you bug me when you don't answer me or when you play dumb about something I'm telling you.

He: It feels like you're pushing me for quick answers. It takes me a little time to think about what you're asking.

She: Well, I thought you'd be pleased that I changed the date for the dinner party like you asked. But you were reluctant to say so, like you had to think it over and drag your feet to get even with me.

He: You're too sensitive. Sure, I do think you take over our calendar too much at times. But, if you remember, I also told you I was glad you had taken care of that.

She: And it bothered me when you asked me for the spare tire for the bike. I had already given it to you, and I couldn't believe you had forgotten that.

He: You forget things too. I wish you weren't so impatient and that you would respect me more.

She: Well, anyway, it feels good to be with you tonight. I've been looking forward to it all day.

He: Me too. I'd like to get to bed early so we can cuddle. It feels good just to be with you.

She: I appreciate the good dinner you fixed tonight. It was great coming home and finding it ready.

He: And I appreciate your cleaning up afterward. When we're both around the kitchen together, it's the most fun.

She: It bothers me that Sarah hung around the house all day and didn't go looking for a job. I'm glad you're talking to her about it; you used to leave it up to me, and I felt like the "heavy."

He: Well, don't worry, honey, I'm in there with you. It bothers me too, and I'm feeling good about speaking up.

A good 15-minute talk can be very satisfying. It's not the quantity of time but the quality that counts. However, other situations need to be confronted as they come up. For example, Hank comes home from the office and excitedly tells Angie about another great investment deal which he just heard about. He grabs the checkbook and walks out the door saying he needs to get to the broker's office before five o'clock. He's gone before she can object.

Angie is upset. She wants Hank to know how important it is for her to decorate the house and take nice vacations. She wants them to travel around the world some day. She appreciates that Hank is good with investments and has their security as a top priority. But she thinks he's too controlling with their money and not willing to take her opinion seriously. He's quick to spend money on an investment but hardly ever willing to pay for some of the things Angie would like them to enjoy.

Angie decides that she must confront Hank with her feelings as soon as he gets home: *Tell my husband that I resent that he doesn't take into account what I want to spend money on (trips and furniture), while he is eager to spend money on what he thinks is important (investments).*

She carefully thinks through her argument. She will talk

to Hank without attacking him. She will tell him from her heart how much her ideas for enjoying their life together mean to her. She won't be defensive, but she will make sure he knows where she's coming from. When Hank returns home, Angie invites him to join her at the kitchen table for coffee and this talk:

Angie: Hank, you have always been an excellent provider for us, and I appreciate how you manage our money.

Hank: What are you leading up to?

Angie: I want to talk about some ways I would like to spend our money.

Hank: This is a bad time to spend money! We are doing a good job of putting God first and taking care of our obligations. I feel strongly that we need to be good stewards of the rest of the money by investing it to grow for our future. Most people don't plan for their retirement years, and they have to keep working or become a burden to their family.

Angie: I would like us to plan in such a way that we have more cash on hand for emergency use. Then I would like some money allowed for redecorating the house and taking some trips. I agree with what you said about being good stewards. It's a matter of degree. I think we should be able to enjoy it as we go, too. I agree we shouldn't be materialistic but we also need to trust God's provision for us. How much money is enough?

Hank: This investment I'm making is very promising. I want to keep all the money I can in there at this time.

Angie: That's what you always say. I have the feeling that there will never be a right time. We have worked long and hard, and we don't know how many more years we will be healthy and able to enjoy ourselves. I think we need to find a balance so we're not continually waiting for some nebulous time to enjoy ourselves.

Hank: You ask for too much sometimes. We have our

future to consider too. I feel like if I give an inch you'll take a mile.

Angie: I don't want to do anything drastic. You can trust me. I want us to do some gradual planning. I'd like to be able to sit down and have some respectful discussions like this so we can influence each other. Doesn't it sound like fun to have the house looking fresh and to take some time off together?

Hank: Sure, I would like that too—eventually. But our house looks nice, and we already take vacations! You need to give credit for what we're already doing. I *do* think it's a good idea to have some money talks. I listen to you, Angie.

Angie: This feels good. I want to work *with* you, not *against* you. I liked what Larry Burkett said about the need for agreement between spouses about money as confirmation from the Lord.

Angie and Hank were both pleased with the confrontation. Both felt they had a good discussion and that they were listening to each other. As they talked, they became more and more reasonable. They could see they weren't so far apart on what they wanted. Both were confident they could talk without being overruled by the other. After their discussion they had weekly finance talks which lead into quarterly joint planning sessions. They developed a mutually beneficial "partnership."

The Fifteen Percent Factor

In all our close relationships, we need to spend about fifteen percent of our waking hours together checking out our feelings with each other. About eighty-five percent of our time can be spent in our thoughts and activities. We need to get our work done and have time to be alone or side by side. But we should reserve fifteen percent to talk about how we are getting along and how we feel about it. Too much can be exhausting and too little leaves us lonely and restless.

You will notice that when you get into the pattern of sharing your feelings in your intimate relationship, fifteen percent of the time will not seem like enough. You may find it difficult to stop talking. But don't go overboard and expand the time. Too much of a good thing will wear you out. Save some sharing for the next time.

Remember: The biggest obstacle to sharing your feelings in your relationships is fear. But each time you push through the fear you will reap rewards. You will feel closer to those you love and stronger about yourself. The fifteen percent of our time we spend discussing feelings adds zest to our lives.

Chapter Nine

Confront Your Anger and Its Allies

"Be imitators of God, therefore, as dearly beloved children. . . . Submit to one another out of reverence for Christ."

Ephesians 5:1, 21

Mary and Dawn had been co-workers and friends for six years. As Mary walked into Dawn's office after work one day, she had something she needed to get off her chest.

"Dawn, it bothers me that you never sit with me and talk with me when we're around other people."

"That's true, Mary," Dawn replied. "I'm often at the other end of the table when we're in a group. I feel like we see each other a lot at work, so I take you for granted."

"I don't want you to take me for granted," Mary stated firmly. "I don't want to have just a work relationship. We say we are friends; I'd like to feel that we are. But you hardly ever initiate our activities together. You've been to our house for dinner several times, but you've only had us over once. I'd like to be invited to your house for dinner more often."

"I've been wanting to ask you to dinner anyway," Dawn answered. "But I keep thinking you won't want to drive all the way out to our place. Mainly, I feel inadequate about having you over for dinner. It's a lot of work for me, and I feel tense about entertaining."

"I have those same feelings about having company," Mary admitted. "Keep the dinner simple. I'd like you to feel at ease around me. Maybe you are uncomfortable around me because I'm so much older than you. Your other friends are closer to your age."

"No, that's not it," Dawn insisted. "Sometimes I think you're too serious, though. I'd like you to loosen up, have more fun and not act so perfect all the time. The more human you are with me, the better I like you."

It is both exciting and frightening when you and your friends open up to each other like Mary did to Dawn. In honest confrontation you know you are going to say—and hear—the truth, the whole truth and nothing but the truth.

Sometimes we prefer our fantasy worlds where our friends are always impressed by us, always agree with us and always like us. But when my friends confront me, I know they see through my exterior to the real me. They see the awkwardness and insecurity that I thought I had hidden so well. And I must remind myself that my friends are showing their true friendship when they speak honestly with me about my flaws. Their confrontations help me stay in touch with the real me and, as a result, help me accept myself for who I am. Yes, we are better people thanks to the good friends who express their feelings to us.

Rehearse Your Confrontations

Confronting someone with your anger is never easy. But you can prepare yourself for the experience and alleviate your fear by rehearsing your confrontation with a trusted friend. The old saying, "Two heads are better than one," is never more true than when applied to discussing an upcoming confrontation. For example, Sally and Terry are discussing Sally's need to confront her husband Cal:

Sally: I need to talk to Cal again about his drinking. I

notice he's not sticking with his commitment of two beers a night. It's creeping up on him again. But I dread saying anything. He gets so defensive.

Terry: I'm sure he does! I think it's important that you bring it up when he's not drinking.

Sally: That would have to be in the morning. When he comes in at night he goes straight to the refrigerator.

Terry: Okay, so you sit down with him in the morning. Keeping it simple, what would you say to him?

Sally: I'd say, "I would like you to stick with your two-beers-a-day commitment."

Terry: That sounds straightforward. If you don't go any further, you've already said the most important thing.

Sally: I can just picture him exploding and yelling at me, "Don't tell me what to do!"

Terry: Then what would you do?

Sally: I'd feel scared and hurt, and I'd probably yell back.

Terry: I think it would be much better just to tell him that you feel scared and hurt! You don't have to be tough with him or try to match his anger.

In rehearsing her confrontation with Terry, Sally reaped the benefits of feedback *before* the event. Sally's regular pattern was to get into a shouting match with Cal instead of swallowing her pride and admitting that she was hurt and afraid of him. It probably would have happened again if she had not talked to Terry first. But Terry, with a more objective view of the relationship, could see that Sally needed to be more vulnerable with Cal if she wanted to get through to him. Their conversation improved Sally's chances of a positive, fruitful confrontation with her husband.

Hurt and Warmth: Anger's Allies

We have explored in depth the feeling of anger and the ramifications of expressing anger in our relationships. But anger is only one of three primary feelings which also include hurt and warmth. It is important to remember that there is dynamic interplay between anger, hurt and warmth. Let's explore the relationship between anger and its two closest allies.

When you have expressed your anger deeply and effectively in a relationship, you will experience hurt and, after a period of time, warmth and closeness with that person. When anger turns to hurt during a fight, let it be a clue that it is time to stop fighting and to ponder what has happened. Feelings of hurt are a buffer zone between anger and warmth, a time for growth as we learn new things about ourselves. It is important that we eventually share our hurt with the person who hurt us and with others who are close to us. Expressing our hurt leads to warmth and closeness.

Feelings of warmth in a relationship are wonderful, and we enjoy basking in them. But sometimes warmth can be difficult to accept. It's often hard for us to believe that we deserve warmth and love in a relationship when it happens, even though we yearn for it all our lives. Also, we fear that the warmth may be pulled out from under us, so we sometimes sabotage it ourselves by leaping back into anger.

It's true: we cannot hang onto feelings of warmth and love perpetually. They come and go throughout life like hurt and anger do. It is important to accept and enjoy each feeling as it comes and live fully in the feelings of the moment without fearing the future or lamenting the past. If you allow yourself to experience what is happening as it happens, the joys will outweigh the sorrows.

But you can block the experience of these feelings in your life. You must consciously *allow* yourself to feel hurt and warmth. And the depth to which you allow yourself to feel and express your anger will determine the depth of your feelings of hurt and warmth. So if you want the full complement of warmth and closeness in your relationship, you must allow yourself to experience the full complement of anger and hurt.

Getting Beneath the Surface

The most important part of expressing our feelings is getting beneath the surface level of conversation at which we usually feel comfortable. We want to be able to make angry statements when previously we were always "nice" to people by withholding our true feelings. We want to express more than the polite "right words" when we are experiencing deep thoughts and feelings.

What we are ultimately after is a deeper level of caring and sharing. We want to feel satisfied that we are achieving honest closeness in our relationships. Such satisfaction results from living on the growing edge of our relationships—being spontaneous and vulnerable and risking our partner's reaction to honest sharing.

When we are really true to ourselves, our deep thoughts and feelings are in tune with the words that come out of our mouths. There is a freedom and an exhilaration in being around people without trying to be something we're not. At first we may worry about impressing others and gaining approval. But after we begin to disagree with each other our guard begins to drop. Gradually we become willing to talk about our problems and share our hurts. And we are surprised to discover that each time we expose a weakness we are more deeply loved than before.

Finally we begin to blossom. We feel lovable and expansive. Our sense of humor comes to the surface. We feel our oats as we let statements pop out that we would have censored before. We are more ready to take risks. We are not overly concerned with what others think of us. We are having fun feeling good about ourselves and letting our enthusiasm tumble out in the words we utter.

When we begin to trust ourselves and others, our surface politeness and formality fade. There is an attractive easiness about us as we openly express warmth, hurt or anger as the need arises. We can flow with what is happening inside us and combine our thoughts and feelings effortlessly. We can sit down and talk without feeling restless. We don't need our usual crutches of cigarettes, work, projects, TV or alcohol. We can look each other in the eye and know that being together is the most important element of our lives.

When we are in tune with ourselves and others in this way, we are able to look deeply at our lives. We can feel the presence of God and can be aware of how he is directing us. Prayer and daily reading of the Bible help us focus on what is important. Then we feel satisfied and peaceful. As we grow in our relationship with God we find it easier to let people come closer. Also, as we let people come closer we find we are closer to God.

Share With Others

Once you begin to experience the freedom and excitement of expressing your feelings instead of suppressing them, you need to share your enthusiasm with others. Share this book with them, encourage them to read it and tell them about the sections which have been especially meaningful to you. Tell your friends that you intend to express your anger as a means of getting closer to them. Talk specifically about what you mean by "expressing anger well." Tell them what your guidelines are, and listen to what they have to say.

Don't expect a positive response from all your friends. We would like to hear all of them say, "I agree with you, and I'm cheering you on." But some of your friends may have problems with your commitment to anger expression and may disagree with your openness. But don't worry; even their disagreement is a form of support. If a friend is honest enough to disagree with you, that means he thinks enough of you to tell you the truth. You can count on a friend like that.

How should you respond to some of the negative statements your friends may make about anger expression? Here are several negative statements and possible ways you may respond:

Negative statement: Anger just gets people into trouble. I know it has upset me all my life, so I don't want to have anything to do with it.

Possible response: Anger has upset me also. That's why I want to know how to handle it. Otherwise I'll be ducking it all my life. It's a part of us; we can't pretend it doesn't exist.

Negative statement: My parents fought all the time, and I'm not going to live that way.

Possible response: Your parents probably were not good fighters. I'm talking about short fights of only five minutes each with neither person trying to win. Anger is scary when you don't understand good fighting. It takes practice to become respectful and feel positive in a fight.

Negative statement: God told us to turn the other cheek. I don't think he wants us to take it on ourselves to be angry. I think he wants us to leave it up to him. So we should give our anger to God instead of expressing it.

Possible response: I believe God will help us with our anger, but he won't take control of our anger for us. We are in charge of our own lives, and we need to take care of our own anger. Ephesians 4:26-27 instructs us to be angry but not to hang onto it. Ephesians 4:31 balances the point by telling us not to go overboard in our anger but to be moderate in its expression and let it go.

Negative statement: I just want to have a good time with you. I don't want things to get heavy by bringing anger to the surface. Can't we just get together and enjoy ourselves?

Possible response: I would like to have a deeper relationship, too. I don't want to be so superficial that we have to be on our best behavior around each other. I agree that we need to have a good time. But I think we also need to say what bothers us and then drop it.

Over the years I have been constantly challenged by friends on the validity of expressing anger. I have become increasingly less defensive as I have become more confident in the need for and rewards of anger expression. I have gravitated toward people who are willing to join me in expressing anger as it arises. Why bang my head against a brick wall? I used to pick the most challenging people to befriend, feeling responsible to put myself and my convictions to the acid test in my friendships. But now I believe that I deserve friends who respect me, appreciate what I am doing and believe in expressing their feelings as a way of life.

I hope you also select some friends to share with you who are open to your ideas and who will practice being honest with you in disagreements. You also need honest friends as sounding boards for handling confrontational situations.

Here's an example of how two friends shared with each other:

Sara: I want to be more myself with my family. Sometimes when I bring up something which needs to be confronted Brian and the kids roll their eyes, and I get cold feet. They all are only too glad to pass over confrontation by changing the subject.

Margie: I know what you mean! Sometimes I plan ahead for something I want to bring up with my mother, trying to build up my determination. But when Mom and Dad get here, it never seems like the right time. First Mom and I are catching up on the news and being friendly. Then we're in the kitchen mashing the potatoes and making the gravy. Then, before you know it, it's time for them to go home, and I don't want them to leave on the sour note of an angry confrontation.

Sara: I have all those rationalizations, too. When I want to tell my sister Betty why I think it is important for Bart and her to have a child, I already know she will be uptight with me for bringing up the subject. I know I should bring it up with Bart there, but then they'll *both* be mad at me. What I'm saying is that I feel so insecure that I'm afraid to do it. Yet I want to be closer to my family than anyone else.

Margie: I know. Yet if we can't say what we're really thinking to our families, we're doomed to feel like polite strangers around them.

Sara: Maybe that's why I'm insecure. I keep thinking my family will reject me. So if I think my family will reject me, how can I believe that anyone else will like me?

Margie: Well, don't get too down on yourself. I think we're both doing better, and all we need to do is include a little more honest talk each time we see our families.

Sara: I'll cheer you on if you'll cheer me on. And you're right. I won't make my lack of progress such a big deal. Most of the time I need to relax and have fun with my family. I just need to say a few things.

By making up your mind that it is good to share your anger appropriately and by talking about it with your family and friends, you will be able to take some positive steps toward improving your relationships. With experience you will increase your ability to flow with your feelings of anger, hurt and love. As it becomes familiar you will find yourself speaking up with ease. This will lead to a fulfilling way of life.

Over the years you will delve gradually deeper into your feelings, and they will become your friends. You can harness them, and they will work for you. You will then feel satisfied with yourself and with those you care for in a way you've never known before. This is what God wants for us.

Chapter Ten

Beyond Anger

"For this reason a man will leave his father and mother and be united to his wife, and the two will become one flesh."

Ephesians 5:31

Now that we have accepted anger as a necessary ingredient in any good relationship and have practiced using good fight rules, what lies ahead for us? Are we going to confront and be confronted endlessly? Will every day bring a round of arguments? If so, I would want to distance myself from friends who are quick to confront me over every little thing.

That's because even though I am familiar with anger and feel equipped to handle it, I do not enjoy it. I tolerate it. I appreciate the strength I feel from expressing it and the good conversations that open up because of it. I see anger taking me deeper into my feelings and hurt and then leading me to love. Because I see the rewards, I'm willing to argue—but I will never relish anger.

It is not fun to have someone you care about tell you what they don't like about what you are doing. Fortunately, with practice, we learn to take anger in stride more easily. Paradoxically, the more we relax about anger the less we are inclined to argue.

When we become good fighters we feel less angry.

Knowing we have the skill to express disagreement well helps us remove the chips from our shoulders. We no longer have to prove something. Finally, we are able to understand these words: "My dear brothers, take note of this: Everyone should be quick to listen, slow to speak and slow to become angry, for man's anger does not bring about the righteous life that God desires." (James 1:19, 20). Rather than bringing up every little thing that bothers us, we need to sort out the major issues and concentrate on those. Then peace will gradually descend on our relationships.

When we do this we can spend most of our time enjoying the people in our lives and spend only a small portion on the anger and hurt that emerge in the course of our days. When we do need to speak out and be vulnerable we know how to keep it simple and accomplish our goal in a short time. Often only a few minutes will be needed for a constructive argument.

Working On Our Relationships: Rolling Up Our Sleeves

Good relationships don't happen naturally. We are all far from perfect and too self-centered to form successful relationships on our own. To understand and improve the ways we express ourselves with those we love we must rely on God's grace and our own continuous effort. This gives us plenty to work on for the rest of our lives, for we never finish improving.

Life is a great challenge as we seek to follow God's Word and cherish the people around us as God wants us to do. Because being honest with our anger enables us to know each other, it helps us begin to understand God's unconditional love for us. It feels wonderful to be accepted for who we are, flaws and all. We can relax and be ourselves and feel we are good enough to be lovable. If we are willing to be honest and listen to the feedback we get, we can admit our mistakes, repent and set about correcting what we have done wrong. Throughout the process we are lovable. We have no need to be defensive. Confrontation, therefore, helps us improve and grow closer to each other. It is not intended for condemnation.

The Transforming of Our Relationship: Twenty Years of Honest Effort

Jack and I have loved each other since our middle teens. Our relationship has been volatile, but we have endured extensive change during our thirty-seven years of marriage. Several times our love was buried under a pile of resentments. Divorce seemed to be the only solution. Each time we were about to give up, God saved us through prayer. His Word spoke to us through our family, friends and good counselors.

The transformation of our relationship was so thrilling to me that I felt called to counsel others who have been unable to find the closeness they desperately want in their relationships. The more I teach, the more I understand the reality of God's power and love. I have also learned my responsibility in developing a joyful intimacy.

Traveling from Fantasy to Reality

I remember how excited I was to become Mrs. Jack Wilson on my wedding day. As we drove off on our honeymoon I daydreamed about what my married life would be like. We would never have to be apart again, and now I had a secure identity in being a wife. I felt confident that Jack loved me so much that he would be a constant support for me. Since he loved me almost as much as he loved himself I knew he would protect me from the world and not allow me to be hurt.

Before long my ideal vision of marriage began to dim. We had bad arguments that left us feeling alienated from each other. We had moved 3,000 miles away from our families and hardly knew anyone in California. I felt desolate. Because I felt dependent on Jack, my whole world darkened when he was angry with me.

Our arguments were awful. I would nag, and he would blow up. Sometimes he would storm out of our apartment and be gone for over an hour. I would cry and become hysterical. Nothing would be resolved so I would punish him by being cold for days on end. We both ended up feeling hurt and a little less trusting of each other. We didn't know how to improve our arguing so we kept repeating the same disastrous patterns, each time damaging our relationship a little more.

We started as one body, but through undisciplined arguing we drifted apart. I felt betrayed because Jack did not respond to my needs as I wanted him to. Assuming that he knew what I wanted, I waited for him to come to me to apologize and hug me and tell me everything would be alright. I certainly didn't think I should have to tell him—if I did tell him then his reaction would seem fake to me. I'm sure that at the same time Jack was waiting for me to come to him in a soft way. We had many such lengthy, hurtful stand-offs.

We unfortunately believed there were only two sides to our arguments: one right, the other wrong. Each of us set out to prove the other person wrong by making a list of the other person's character defects. A power struggle ensued. Since we were both strong and stubborn we became adept at putting each other down. It was frustrating, though, because neither of us could claim a clear-cut victory. We began to speak critically of each other to our friends. This made us drift further apart.

The fighting between us was only making our lives worse, yet we felt helpless. Neither of us had ever seen a good, constructive argument to know such a thing existed. Over the next fifteen years we muddled along, experimenting with different ideas about how to make things better. Many times Jack tried to appease me but eventually he would reach the end of his rope and explode. (I vividly remember a table flying across the room on one occasion.) I also tried to please Jack, rushing home to fix his lunch right on the dot of noon everyday. Eventually, though, I would be sick to death of doing things I didn't really feel like doing, and I would harshly tear him down and let him know I didn't respect him.

We drifted ever farther apart, doing separate things, seeing separate friends, keeping our separate thoughts. Sex fell apart and the bedroom became a battleground. We began to threaten each other. We were attracted to other people.

My sister and brother-in-law came to visit and pleaded with us to talk to our minister. We did, and this was the beginning of a long series of counselors and teachers who taught us how to express our anger constructively.

At first we felt worse rather than better. Having the truth out in the open was painful and stirred up our anger. We had to get rid of our secrets if we were to give each other an honest chance of getting close. Because we were taking these big risks we often felt scared and upset.

We had spent years letting our anger build up to the point where we sought help, and we were unable to change overnight. Patience did not come naturally for either Jack or me, but we prayed for it and learned to accept small, steady steps in the right direction.

Part of being patient was finding out how to weather hurt. That had been our sticking point for a long time. Both Jack and I liked to stay angry rather than feel hurt. When I was deeply hurt I would threaten to divorce Jack. That threat would keep me self-righteously indignant so I wouldn't feel sad.

I vividly remember one night we went to see our counselor, John. We had been arguing a lot, blaming each other, and once again I was threatening to break up our relationship.

John turned to me and said, "Ruth, I am tired of your

166 / The Gift of Anger

threats. I have been with you and Jack long enough to know you love each other. I think you have picked each other for good reasons and I think you are wasting time with this bad fighting.

"I want you to make a commitment tonight never to use the word 'divorce' with each other again. Furthermore, rather than coming to group tonight, I want the two of you to go out and have a quiet dinner together."

We made that commitment, and I remember what a quiet, hurt dinner it was! Without my "escape hatch" (threat) I had no where to go except to feel hurt. Would Jack really care for me? Could we ever trust each other again? Could we forgive each other and be close?

If we were staying together, we had to improve the quality of our relationship. We both set about with new vigor to make things better between us. From that night on I learned to sit quietly with my hurt and learn from it, which gave me an endurance that had been missing.

We had to work through many difficult issues between us: addictions, bad fighting habits, low self esteem, problems from our original families and lack of faith in God. Progress was slow but continuous until we felt reborn in our relationship.

Today, after 20 years of learning and practicing being open and direct with each other, Jack and I are deeply in love in a way we never felt before. We feel the special bond of attraction we felt in the beginning plus the depth and rich-ness of all our years together. We definitely are one body as God intended us to be.

We tell each other everything, and there is an intimacy in knowing all about each other. We are willing to risk because we know how to argue and we can weather that; we know about hurt and we can bounce back from that; and we are secure. The bottom line in our relationship is that we love each other and that makes the anger and hurt worthwhile.

There is a freedom in this ability to trust our feelings with each other. We are able to say honestly what we think, feel and want, knowing we will be loved no matter what. We care so much about each other, we *want* to please each other. From that perspective our arguments are easier and easier to resolve. When we argue we think about respecting and listening to each other. We are aware we're each making good points, and we are going to learn something important. On big issues we plan to have forty-five five-minute discussions, knowing anything can be resolved with that much effort. Often it only takes a few talks!

For example, recently Jack and I made plans to go to Thailand, but the trip was canceled on the final sign-up day for lack of subscription. Here is our first five-minute discussion:

"I'm so disappointed the trip has been canceled," I said. "We went back and forth on it so much—then we finally decide 'yes' and it's called off!"

"It's interesting that a lot of other people were complaining about too much flying time, just as I was," Jack replied. "We'll come up with something else—I'll check with Kathryn at the travel agency."

"I blocked off the time in February, and I was telling everyone about it. It'll be hard to get a trip together to go at that same time, but I'd like to try," I added.

"Let's see how it works out. It might be better to go in September since we have two trips this spring," said Jack.

"I don't want to give up on it so quickly. February is summer down below. How about New Zealand?" I pressed.

"We were not intended to go on this trip. Let's see what God provides, Ruth."

"Well I want us to do our part too, Jack. Will you call Kathryn tomorrow?"

"Tomorrow will be a *busy* day for me," said Jack. "I'll call her on Friday."

We stopped at that point. I was feeling frustrated because

I wasn't getting the response I wanted from Jack, but I knew it would do no good to go further. We had both given our opinions, and it was time to mull them over.

From this conversation it's clear Jack is more flexible than I am. I love to be organized, to plan and anticipate. This time the rug had been pulled out from under me. Jack heard, though, how important taking a trip at this time would be for me. I knew he would carefully consider what I wanted. I trusted our future talks would resolve the problem.

Above all, Jack and I know we must reach agreement on major decisions. We understand we are intended to be a team and that the two of us equal much more than the sum of one and one. Consulting goes on in all areas of our life. We plan our overall investing program, how many nights we are willing to be out, how much to spend on a birthday gift, what kind of food we want to eat, when to call our children, what service to attend at church, etc., etc., etc.!

Our expectations and roles have changed. Since we no longer compete to be right or on top there is more mutual encouragement. Either of us can do any job around the house. Whoever has the time or who wants to do the task the most takes it on. Extra care is automatically given to the one who may be tired, sick or under stress. We don't keep a score card. Rather, there is generous giving from a full heart.

Growing older together brings out our tenderness. We do not take little things for granted. We cuddle in bed, bring each other a cup of coffee and sit side-by-side eating our morning bowl of hot cereal that we take turns fixing for each other. Jack will pump up my bike tires. Together we make the bed, talking all the while about our plans for the day. We determine who will be able to make the bank deposit or pick up a few groceries; often we are both willing, and we may fight for the privilege. Finally, the moment comes when we leave for the day. We hug each other and pray for each other's welfare that day. Nothing is sweeter in life than tender moments with the person dearest to us.

Whoever would have thought that the later years in life could be the most passionate—yet for us they are. Sex has reached a quality of love that is unsurpassed. We reach for each other with the tender desire to be one body. We relish the closeness God has allowed us. We are genuinely solicitous of each other's needs. If one of us does not reach an orgasm we can smile about it and give a hug. Most times orgasms happen easily and are not the most important part. Either of us can initiate sex and most often the other wants to say "yes."

We have not become angels yet, however. Sometimes we slip back into our old ways. Usually this happens when we are tired or under stress. After all, our basic personalities have not changed, although we have learned to modify them with God's help. But now we catch ourselves sooner, are more ready to admit our mistakes and are not willing for a bad moment to hang around for any length of time to spoil our fun. We know a better way of talking and arguing.

No matter who is around we put each other first. When our grown children and our grandchildren come to see us we do not drop each other in the excitement. Because we are off balance in the commotion, it takes extra effort to seek each other out to give information and a hug. But we feel better when we do, and our children appreciate seeing us that way. Because we've come a long way we can be good models for them. What greater encouragement can there be for marriage than seeing your over-fifty-year-old parents in love?

We used to be afraid to take the risk of being angry because we might be rejected. Now we face a new risk from our closeness: We fear we will suddenly lose each other. Because we love each other so much and have come to rely on our warmth and companionship, we are afraid we will be devastated when one of us dies.

Each year we take a trip to Maui where we own a condominium.We look forward all year to going away together to our heaven on earth. We both work hard in our everyday lives so we especially thrive on the peaceful time of unwinding together without pressures on us.

From the time we get off the plane and the tropical breeze hits our faces, we slow down. Everyday we wake up without an alarm clock. We start the day by talking in bed. We mosey peacefully through our day together: swimming, reading, jogging, shopping, dozing, snorkeling, eating, and talking and talking.

We used to worry that we might get bored. Instead, as time goes by our enjoyment grows. The quality of our conversation changes. Instead of having to fill each other in on what we have missed we are now reacting in the moment to what we are experiencing together. We have time to reflect and share aloud our thoughts.

The conversation can be light and fun or deep and serious. Sometimes we argue, but it is quick and clean. We are not afraid to disagree since we know the limits and that the fight is temporary. During the last trip we talked about the meaning of our lives and talked from the depth of our beings about God. Finally, toward the end of our trip, we reached our closest moments. Our fear of losing each other surfaced. We poured out our hearts to each other as we never have before.

"I am having such a perfect time with you that I feel reluctant to give it up to go home. Life seems so simple here, and I can really appreciate how much I love you and enjoy your company," Jack said.

"I've been thinking the same way. I start planning how we can keep these peaceful warm feelings going. I find myself planning how to keep our lives simpler and more focused on each other. I thought we might get bored at some point, but it only seems to get better," I replied.

"Every year I start to think about retiring and living here at least part of the year. We'd have no trouble finding enough to do. You could do some writing, and I could spend time studying the stock market," Jack continued.

"I let myself play with the idea, too! Then I think I can't be gone so long from our children and grandchildren and the others we love. And I'm not sure God wants us to take it that easy. I think we have more to do for him. When I feel sad about leaving I remember that we get to go home *together,* and we have a good life there," I said.

"What I notice is I feel so tender and caring of you and then I feel afraid . . . afraid that our relationship is so good it will be snatched away. I'm not afraid of death as much as I am of leaving you. I trust God that heaven will be all I could ever want, yet I don't want to say 'goodbye' to you," Jack added, tears in his eyes.

"I don't like it that there is no marriage in heaven, but I do have to trust God. I've been afraid I couldn't bounce back from the pain of losing you. I have been with you for most of my life. I can hardly remember a time without you. You hear a lot about one spouse dying and within a few months the other follows. Mom and Dad were like that. They were so devoted to each other they didn't want to go on alone. Yet I think the children will need the one who survives. It's so sad and yet so beautiful. I love you so much!" I said, with tears flowing.

"I think God has given us a great blessing that we have had each other for such a long time. Don't worry; we will survive the hurt and recover. We are both strong, and God will not give us more than we can bear. We need to put him first in our life. Everything we have comes from him," Jack said.

"I do finally feel he is there continuously and that he will never let me down," I replied. "No matter what happens to either of us he will comfort us. I see how great is his love for us. I also see the more I love God the more I love you . . . and the more I love you the more I love God. I feel deep joy."

Jack and I kissed each other and embraced.

God wants his love to be reflected into the world through our relationships. The first step is honest, caring confrontation. I pray you'll take that first step today.